Praise for *The Effort Myth*

What can you do when your child has lost motivation? *The Effort Myth* is the guided journey that you need to get and stay on track. Sherri Fisher's practical approach is both easy to understand and implement for parents trying to do what is best for their child to thrive beyond schoolwork to lifetime learning. Through humorous and poignant stories, Fisher's practical parenting and learning strategies help you to see your struggling child and yourself in liberating, positive, and constructive ways. I will find myself revisiting this work to provide support academically and socially while we, as parents, create a foundation for our lifelong learners.

Ari Abramson
Vice-President, Acquisitions
Continental Realty Corporation
Former student, current (parent)
client, and lifelong learner

In *The Effort Myth*, Sherri begins at the heart of it all – the parent-child relationship. With clarity, empathy, and humor, she shares concrete coaching strategies and questions that will transform how parents communicate with their children. It is from within this fortified parent-child partnership that any parents can give their children the gifts of competence, choices, and self-direction.

Lauren Killeen, PhD
Pediatric Neuropsychologist, Parent
Social Emotional Educational &
Developmental Services (SEEDS)

The Effort Myth is Sherri Fisher's best book yet. Sherri shows us that education is not a one-size-fits-all endeavor and that each child can learn how to learn. I wish that *The Effort Myth* was available when I was growing up and later when raising my own children. I highly recommend this for parents, teachers, and adults who themselves were challenged learners. Using well-founded research and years of experience as a coach and educator, Sherri's approach is personal, engaging, and accessible. I even walked away with some powerful learning about myself!

Sandy Lewis, PCC
President, Positive Shift Coaching

The world of education and learning seems a lot more complicated than it was when today's parents were students. In this book, Sherri Fisher busts the "effort myth" – that admonishing kids to "just try harder" is the answer when they are struggling in school. If that sounds like your child, you want Fisher on your team. This book is the next best thing.

Jenny Lisk
Author of *Future Widow* and host of
The Widowed Parent Podcast

The Effort Myth is chock full of great student-empowerment tools for parents and educators alike! I'm even going to encourage my own two college-age children to read it. The useful tips and insights can help them strengthen their own learning journeys!

Kathy Snyder
High School Teacher, Retired
Coordinator of the Midland Area
Wellbeing Coalition

The Effort Myth is like finding a best friend to help you through the troubled waters and challenges of parenting kids who struggle in school. It's full of helpful insights and wisdom told in story form. If I had but one wish for all my fellow parents and friends it would be to share this book. Sherri Fisher is a gift to us all.

Kevin Rea, Founder,
Rea Company Homes
Builder of The Year,
Custom Builder Magazine

Give the Three Gifts of Motivation

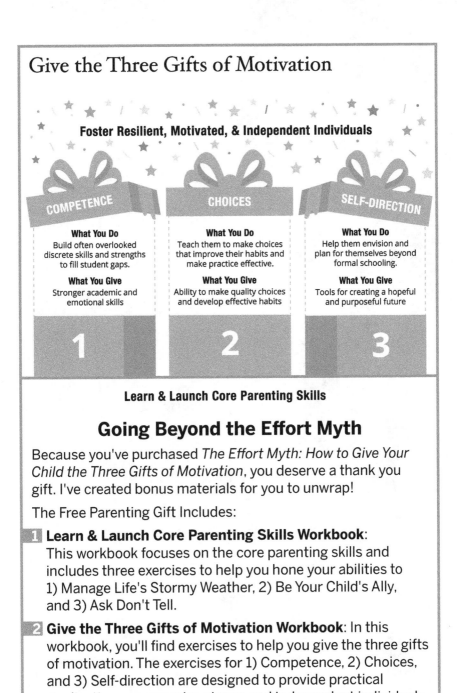

Foster Resilient, Motivated, & Independent Individuals

COMPETENCE

What You Do
Build often overlooked discrete skills and strengths to fill student gaps.

What You Give
Stronger academic and emotional skills

1

CHOICES

What You Do
Teach them to make choices that improve their habits and make practice effective.

What You Give
Ability to make quality choices and develop effective habits

2

SELF-DIRECTION

What You Do
Help them envision and plan for themselves beyond formal schooling.

What You Give
Tools for creating a hopeful and purposeful future

3

Learn & Launch Core Parenting Skills

Going Beyond the Effort Myth

Because you've purchased *The Effort Myth: How to Give Your Child the Three Gifts of Motivation*, you deserve a thank you gift. I've created bonus materials for you to unwrap!

The Free Parenting Gift Includes:

1 **Learn & Launch Core Parenting Skills Workbook**: This workbook focuses on the core parenting skills and includes three exercises to help you hone your abilities to 1) Manage Life's Stormy Weather, 2) Be Your Child's Ally, and 3) Ask Don't Tell.

2 **Give the Three Gifts of Motivation Workbook**: In this workbook, you'll find exercises to help you give the three gifts of motivation. The exercises for 1) Competence, 2) Choices, and 3) Self-direction are designed to provide practical applications as you raise strong and independent individuals.

Simply go to **www.theeffortmyth.com/bookgifts** to sign up for your free parenting gifts.

(I'd love to keep in touch with you. And don't worry—Your contact information will never be sold or shared with anyone, and you can unsubscribe at any time.)

the Effort Myth

How to Give Your Child the
Three Gifts of Motivation

SHERRI W. FISHER

PositiveEdgePress

The Effort Myth

© 2021 by Sherri W. Fisher

 Published by Positive Edge Press
PositiveEdgePress Medfield MA

ISBN 978-1-7321368-1-6 (paperback)
ISBN 978-1-7321368-2-3 (eBook)

Library of Congress Control Number: 2021919451

Disclaimer:
The advice and strategies found within may not be suitable for every situation. This book is designed to provide general educational information about the subjects discussed and not intended as a substitute for the diagnosis, treatment, cure, or prevention of any social, physical, psychological, or emotional condition, or as a substitute for the professional advice of a physician, psychologist, psychiatrist, or other expert's direct assistance.

Use of this book does not establish any type of advisory, counseling, or professional relationship with the author or publisher. References to other sources are provided for informational purposes only and do not constitute an endorsement of those sources. This work is sold with the understanding that neither the author nor the publisher is held responsible for the results accrued from the advice in this book.

While all attempts have been made to verify information provided for this publication, the publisher assumes no responsibility for errors, omissions, or contrary interpretation of the subject matter herein.

For more information, visit https://theEffortMyth.com.

To my children
For delighting me with your originality
For giving me the opportunity to grow even stronger
For loving me even when I am difficult

Foreword

I first crossed paths with Sherri when she referred an engaging and creative middle school student for a neuropsychological evaluation. He had a history of executive function and language-based learning challenges and was becoming increasingly frustrated, sad, and self-critical. In my role as a pediatric neuropsychologist, I gather insights from the network of allies in a child's life – caregivers, teachers, therapists, learning specialists – and integrate them with assessment data and clinical observation. The goal is to better understand how a child processes academic, social, and emotional information.

When Sherri and I connected to discuss this particular student, I was immediately struck by her ability to see the child *between* the data. She is incredibly skilled at pinpointing and translating a child's information-processing style into real world applications. Sherri envisions what it must be like to walk in a child's shoes given their unique profile of strengths and challenges. It is from that place of empathetic understanding that she builds a meaningful action plan to help students leverage their strengths to thrive not only in learning, but also in life.

Roughly 5%-15% of school-age children have a specific learning disorder in reading, writing, and/or mathematics, and about 5% of children have attention and executive function impairments. These students are at increased risk for school dropout, psychological distress, poorer overall mental health, and unemployment or under-employment. However, high levels of social and emotional support serve as protective factors, leading to better mental health outcomes. Sherri is an expert at this intersection, helping children and their families learn and apply the tools they need to develop agency, satisfaction, and joy in the face of challenge.

In the years that I have been fortunate to collaborate with Sherri about our many mutual clients, I have been astonished at how often discouraged, distressed, and seemingly demotivated learners emerge from their work with her with improved well-being, ownership and pride in their strengths. They have gained tangible skills to leverage those strengths in the real world. It is always a joy to hear how students, like the very first middle school child we collaborated over, have gone on to experience successes in higher education, careers, and interpersonal relationships.

In *The Effort Myth*, Sherri begins at the heart of it all – the parent-child relationship. With clarity, empathy, and humor, she shares concrete coaching strategies and questions that will transform how parents communicate with their children. It is from within this fortified parent-child partnership that any parent can give their children the gifts of competence, choices, and self-direction. Readers will find clearly defined skills with real-world examples, step-by-step strategies to address challenges, and organizational tools leading to a comprehensive action plan. Sherri's gift to compassionate and concerned parents and other caregivers is a roadmap for helping children journey toward resilience, motivation, and independence.

Lauren A. Killeen, Ph.D., Fall 2021
Pediatric Neuropsychologist
Founder/Director, Social Emotional
Educational & Developmental
Services (SEEDS)

Contents

Figures

Tables

Preface

I remember the moment I became a parent. It was not when I found out that I was pregnant or when I washed and folded tiny clothes from my baby shower. It was not when my first child was born or when I held her for the first time. It was not when I heard her newborn cry or saw her kick the nurses' clipboard from the corner of the isolette where she lay on her back, gazing around the delivery room. Those moments were all very real, but they did not make me feel like a parent.

Feeling like a parent happened one day shortly after my daughter was born. We were passengers in a car driven by someone else. The driver made a right turn onto a familiar street near my neighborhood and then proceeded as if nothing were out of the ordinary. But there it was: the level railroad crossing where the freight train passed by several times a day. For some reason, this drive that I had made safely for years was suddenly fraught with parenthood.

The sense of responsibility I felt at that moment was so weighty and memorable that I can still hear with train-whistle clarity what it sounded like: *You are a child's mother*. This was a moment of great humility that changed me forever. When

I went to the grocery store or saw neighbors with children, I had a new appreciation for hope, love, and frustration. When I returned to work, I found that I had a new lens for teaching. Instead of looking at children as students to teach, I zoomed in: Everybody there was somebody's baby.

My first child was still an infant when I was asked by client parents to attend a public-school IEP meeting with them. I took my new lens to this meeting. Though their child was old enough to be entering high school, earlier private testing had shown 3rd grade independent skills across a number of literacy measures. Now, after only six months of specialized tutoring with me, he tested two grade levels higher. The boy's teachers noticed the difference, but they attributed his improvement to maturity and a willingness to try harder. "See?" one teacher asked his parents. "He really can do it if he tries." Rather than giving them hope, this enraged and insulted the boy's devoted parents. The boy, who was sitting next to me in the meeting, crossed his arms, tucked his chin inside his shirt, and slid way down in his chair.

Like all meetings of this kind, the chairperson began with introductions for invited attendees. All of the school personnel gave their names (made up ones here) and their titles. "Ms. Gold, Speech-Language Pathologist. Ms. Sparks, English-Language Arts Teacher. Mr. Radcliffe, School Psychologist. Mr. Thomas, Principal. Ms. Tyrone, Special Educator. Ms. Olin, Guidance Counselor." After all of them had given name and role, the parents, who had no titles, spoke their names. When it was the boy's turn, he said, "Student."

No one asked me who I was. The mother introduced me by name.

"This woman has changed our son's life," the father added. "She has a gift."

In the context of a meeting in which I was advocating for them, this family shone a light on me. I humbly vowed to support them and their son. I knew even then, in my twenties, that effort alone could not turn around a struggling learner. I now understood that I was on team Whatever-It-Takes. No child on my watch would have to suffer to access their learner's birthright.

This boy was the first of nearly a thousand children I have since successfully represented at special education meetings. I have offered my gifts to thousands more who did not need special education but who did need the gifts of motivation. I have devoted my professional life to living up to one parent's description of me, "TOTAL: All the ingredients you need."

I have founded school and academic camp programs to support students and train teachers. As a leading positive psychology practitioner and the first learning specialist to earn the University of Pennsylvania's Master of Applied Positive Psychology (MAPP) degree, I merge my Ivy League graduate education with personalized, down-to-earth, practical learning strategies. Concurrently, I have directed a thriving consulting practice for over 30 years. My clients on five continents include parents, students, schools, other professionals, and an elite international sporting organization.

My work and research have influenced thousands of educators. I co-authored the first book applying positive psychology to education, *SMART Strengths: Building Strengths, Resilience and Relationships*. I have authored or co-authored five other books and written more than 50 research-based articles.

Because I'm always looking for the most up-to-date, effective, and customizable ways to help parents and students, I have worked with pioneers in the fields of dyslexia education, neuropsychology, and positive psychology. I have traveled internationally as an invited speaker at numerous professional conferences and taught positive psychology as a guest lecturer to hundreds of undergraduate and graduate students in the United States, Canada, Mexico, and Australia.

I did not know when I became a parent that all of these opportunities would come my way. When my infant daughter and I were passengers in that car, I experienced profound recognition of great responsibility and overwhelming love. I did not stop with one child. I had another one of my own and have raised up thousands of others to believe in their own gifts of motivation. Whether you are a parent, relative, friend, prospective parent, or teacher, this book can help you learn to give the three gifts of motivation to the students you care about.

Introduction

Has it ever seemed to you that your child spends more effort resisting work than just getting it done? Many parents have sat at their kitchen table, night after night, feeling exasperated as they watch their children not get homework done. They often hear their children yell, "I am trying!" perhaps through tears. It is so tempting to tell them to try harder.

However, the answer is not just to put in more effort. I label this answer *the effort myth.* It is a story that adults tell about a student who seems smart enough to be successful, but who is struggling to achieve, especially in school. "If my child would just try harder..." Like other myths, the effort myth is a widely held belief that is false. Successful students do more than just try. They try differently. I tell the students I coach, "It's not how hard you try that leads to success. It's **how** you try hard." Using the ideas in this book, you can help your children learn how to spend their effort effectively in ways that move them forward.

After showing parents how to develop the skills that make them effective supporters for their children in the education process, this book explores the three primary gifts that parents can give their children to help them become independent, lifelong learners. These gifts are important whether a child is doing well in school or struggling to keep up. They can turn around a downward spiral and help children move ahead, even those with significant learning challenges.

This book has answers for many questions that plague parents. How can you participate effectively in the education of your children? When do you need to step in and when do you need to let your children figure it out themselves? How do you help in ways that enable your children to grow in ability and independence?

Who is This Book For?

This book is for parents and other adults who are looking for answers beyond telling children to try harder. Of course, effort is *necessary* for work to be done successfully. However, trying harder is *not sufficient* by itself. Often, focusing on effort makes motivation problems worse, minimizing a child's real needs, wearing away at their belief in their own abilities, and decreasing their love of learning. They may accumulate fear of not measuring up, which can lead to anxiety. What's also heart-breaking about the "Just try harder" approach is that it can mask students' real strengths, keeping parents and students from seeing what is good and even powerful about them.

Many children struggle in school despite having at least normal intelligence. They may or may not have a learning disability diagnosis or be receiving special help. Their parents can become exasperated because they correctly believe their child is smart enough to do better. This book offers answers to the common parental challenge, "How can I help my child access their smartness?"

In this book I draw on my extensive experience working with clients who have learning, attention, and executive function challenges, as well as with students who need more individualized and purposeful approaches to working than are offered by the general curriculum. Woven throughout this book, I share stories drawn from my decades of work in schools, in private practice as a learning specialist, and as a positive psychology coach for parents. I also bring you my own personal experience as a mother of capable and complicated children.

How is This Book Organized?

This book is divided into two major parts.

Part 1: Core Parenting Skills gives parents new ways to build emotional awareness and practice effective parenting approaches. Part 1 addresses understanding the limitations of the effort myth, building resilience, forming alliances with others, and coaching your child effectively. These skills can help you grow as a parent. Gaining confidence in these skills will give you a firmer foundation to give the gifts described in Part 2.

Part 2: The Three Gifts of Motivation shows you how to give your child what I have found to be the crucial gifts of motivation. The gifts are:

- Competence: Building often overlooked discrete skills to fill student gaps

- Choices: Helping them make choices that improve habits and make practice effective

- Self-direction: Helping them envision themselves beyond formal schooling

When you can spot where these gifts are needed, you can give your child developmentally and emotionally appropriate approaches for learning solid academic skills, developing effective personalized habits, and creating a hopeful, purposeful future.

Inklings are brief stories that follow each chapter. These stories reinforce the message of the preceding chapter and help you embark on envisioning your child's future story. Many of these inklings come from my own story, which certainly did not proceed in a straight line. These true stories about my students and me illustrate the way the foggiest thoughts can become clearer with time and perspective. As your child writes their future story, it helps to be willing to try things out, perhaps abandon them, and later join pieces together that earlier seemed unconnected. Sometimes only upon reflection can a person see what has been there all along.

Who Are the Stories About?

This book is full of stories that draw upon my years of experience. However, in my work it is very important to safeguard confidential client information. Therefore, the stories are works of very realistic fiction. They demonstrate situations that I have observed with client families and students, but no story in this book corresponds to a real person except the stories about me, my children, and Nikhil. Nikhil (not his real name) gave me permission to tell his story as I remembered it because he hoped it would help others.

The stories are composites drawn from the thousands of clients and school children I have known through decades of work. In some cases, I have fictionalized small details to emphasize the relevant points. If you have been my student or a parent, know that I have not described you in this book. If a story sounds like you, remember that many other students and families have stories similar to yours.

In student stories, I have used the pronouns he/his/him, she/hers/her, and they/theirs/them to refer to students as if I had asked them their preference. All of the names, genders, pronouns, story resolutions and other identifying information are my constructions. In the rest of the book, I use they/theirs/them for both plural and singular pronouns.

....

I believe that no one should have to suffer to be an effective learner. Often, children would try harder if they only knew how. Do you want new ways to uncover your child's motivation? You are holding in your hands a book that can turn the effort myth into a story that is *true*, in which your child becomes resilient, motivated, and independent. These are foundations of lifelong learning and success.

Let's get started!

PART 1
....
Core Parenting Skills

Part 1 helps you prepare to give your child the three gifts of motivation. As much as you may want to skip around or go directly to the gifts themselves, I encourage you to start by building your own foundational skills. I will reference these skills over and over throughout the rest of the book, and they can smooth your parenting journey.

It can be easy to see lack of motivation as your child's own problem to fix. The truth is that your child depends on relationships with others, especially with you, to launch the behaviors that lead to independence. Examples of core parenting skills covered in Part 1 include:

- Recognizing when you are falling prey to believing the effort myth and shifting into more productive thinking patterns

- Developing awareness of your own automatic thinking that can fuel emotion storms

- Managing parent peer pressure and social comparison, and detecting beliefs that keep you from allowing your child to take appropriate risks

- Creating emotional safety for your child even when you cannot yield to their wishes

- Learning to ask questions that convey support rather than judgment

- Building relationships with others, including teachers, who can help you on your parent journey

....

CHAPTER 1

Let Go of the Effort Myth

The effort myth broadcasts a false promise of success tinged with fear. Just asking your children to try harder is unlikely to solve their education challenges. This chapter introduces you to related blind spots about what smart really means. It also reinforces that it's not how hard someone tries but _how_ they try hard that makes the difference when it comes to success.

What is The Effort Myth?

A _myth_ is a story that tries to explain the unexplainable. With larger-than-life characters, some of whom have superpowers, myths address the mysteries of creation as well as the tragedies, frustrations, and joys of being human. Myths convey the behavior of paragons and illustrate cultural values such as bravery, loyalty, and sacrifice. Also embedded in myths are warnings about the consequences of yielding to temptation or failing to correct one's flaws. While a myth's facts may be cloudy, the beliefs they convey about fate, responsibility, and choice are usually very clear.

The effort myth that is told about student learning is a story that perpetuates the belief that success is the reliable outcome of trying harder. It also broadcasts a series of warnings:

- If you do not try harder, you may fail.

- If you fail, you will have a less attractive future story.

- If you have a less attractive future story, it may be your own fault.

In this myth, teachers, and sometimes by extension, parents, plead with students to heed their warnings. "I believe in you," they say. "I know you can do it if you try harder," they encourage. Though the intention is to motivate action, the approach can instead discourage it.

The Real Pathway to Learning

Trying the same things that did not work initially over and over with greater energy is not the recipe for success. Repeating the effort myth also obscures the real reasons for life success:

> *Achievement after initial failure lies in being able to try in a new way and to identify sometimes small but not inconsequential differences. That's because trying again and succeeding means that at least something was done differently.*

Instead of a call for more and more effort, students need tools for uncovering what has worked for them. Sometimes they will also need support from adults to learn new skills and develop personalized practices for independence.

The Learner's Birthright: You Should Not Have to Suffer to Learn

Some students grow up without ever feeling that they have struggled in school. Sometimes this is because they do not expect much of themselves. As long as they pass, they feel ok with average grades. They arrive in high school where classes are leveled, and they do not anticipate being in the honors track. College might be in their future, but they won't be applying to extremely selective schools. They might not hate school, but they aren't motivated to change.

A different child, perhaps with learning, attention, and executive function challenges, may have processing and emotional impacts as a result of their learning profile. If they are undiagnosed, their inattention may look as if they actively seek distractions, and their struggles to learn may make it look as if they have stopped caring. They may avoid doing work that parents and teachers are sure they could do if they only tried harder. Students may push back because it feels as if someone is always keeping after them. They feel that their school performance is more important than they are.

As we will explore in this book, the behaviors of a learning- and performance-challenged person are symptoms of underlying challenges, not the actual problem. But the student can *feel* as if they themselves are the problem. The costs of believing in the effort myth, that just trying harder will ultimately lead to success, can be very high. In the absence of knowing how to try more effectively, and without an explanation for their learning difficulties, students who struggle to learn may feel misunderstood. They may be confusing, even to themselves.

Blind Spots About Student Success

Part of the reason that educators rely on the effort myth so much is that they are working with classrooms of students of a certain age, guiding them through a particular curriculum of skills and content. In same-age inclusive groups, students are compared to standards of expected performance with the curriculum. This can lead to blind spots. Here are some mistaken beliefs about the causes of student success:

Blind Spot #1: Some students are smarter than others.

The truth? Smart is not on a ladder and by itself is not a strength. It can be measured many ways. Consider that the same program with agreed-upon content might be taught by instructors with very different approaches and expectations, even when they have standards and rubrics to follow. Attributing success to intelligence misses the possibility that students have been able to thrive because of provided structure, and because the challenges presented by a teacher just happen to meet their talents and skills at a given time.

Blind Spot #2: School success determines life success.

The truth? Students benefit from discovering topics and experiences at school that are engaging and learning that really works for them. However, the ways we choose to measure and reward success are an important part of what makes some people appear more successful than others. Smart is not what a person is. Smart includes believing that there is something else to try and that effort will be worthwhile. There are other contexts besides school where a student may discover their own ability to learn skills and grow the abilities that lead to a meaningful and purposeful life.

Blind Spot #3: Elementary school performance strongly predicts later school performance.

The truth? Students who have done well in the structured elementary school setting are often assumed to be good at efficiently organizing materials, following directions, and managing distractions. When they get to middle school, however, underdeveloped skills, processing challenges, and working memory limitations can challenge their ability to perform up to new standards. Previous star students may then struggle to shine.

Blind Spot #4: Challenges experienced in childhood limit future career paths.

The truth? Success is more about knowing how to leverage non-academic strengths and applying them to a particular setting than about overcoming school challenges. As a professional who has also worked extensively with adolescents bridging the school-to-work transition, I have observed that as people age, they often find themselves drawn to work on challenges that do not require their school weaknesses. Have they outgrown their diagnoses? It may look that way if they seem to struggle less. Perhaps as adults, they have been able to exert more choice to find what constitutes a good fit for themselves, avoiding the challenges of their childhoods.

Barriers to Learning

Some teachers have lots of experience accommodating different learners, both by challenging them and by supporting them. They are flexible and open to trying different approaches, especially in elementary and early middle school. Still, it is widely believed that students cannot learn if they do not do their schoolwork.

Education need not be about creating barriers to learning. Rather than being learning disabled, some children can be environmentally disabled or even teaching-style disabled. Some students know a lot about how they learn best, and they will tell you if you will listen. Many classrooms are overly focused on being places for learning subject-area content mandated by state frameworks. Given that so many topics that students will need to learn in their lifetimes, both content and strategies, have not even been discovered yet, the goal of an education also needs to be weighted toward learning *how* to learn best, and especially to applying strengths and self-knowledge for new learning.

What a person thinks it means to be learning matters. A lot! When students do not seem to be effectively gaining essential content knowledge needed for future school and life success, it can create background noise of great fear in parents. Is their underachieving child setting themselves up for a lifetime of struggle? To become high achievers, students need to become both self-regulated and resilient, skills that can be developed in and out of school.

The Effort Myth in Report Cards

Your child's report cards may even seem to have written proof of the effort myth. According to typical teacher comments from report cards, the simple solution to higher performance and more desirable grades is more effort. Below are actual teacher comments copied from my clients' report cards, though I have changed the student names. Notice how confident the teachers sound in their comments that more student effort is the missing magic ingredient that will yield better student achievement:

- "Kayla does not apply her ability in a consistent manner. With more effort this will change." (grade 6)

- "Jack likes to settle for mediocre work when he is competent to produce amazing work. With more effort and higher expectations of himself this can turn around." (grade 7)

- "It is disheartening that Mira does not take more pride in her work. When she applies more effort, she will improve her grades." (grade 8)

- "Dashiel needs to acquire a different mindset, one conducive to his talents. He just needs to try." (grade 9)

- "Nico's effort has been disappointing this term. She is so talented and capable and should not settle for less than trying to be the best she can be." (grade 10)

- "Milo needs to make an effort to attend after-school help sessions. This will improve his grade." (grade 11)

- "More effort is needed for Avia to reach her potential. I have seen her try some days and believe she can turn things around." (grade 12)

No wonder you are frustrated with your child! The solution to their underachievement is plain and simple, right? Teachers keep telling you that all they have to do is try.

What if You Believe in the Effort Myth?

Do you believe that gritty effort is the key to success? If so, you may believe in the effort myth, too. Many well-meaning parents and teachers try to motivate students by telling them that they just need to try harder. Other respected adults in a student's life also assure them that trying harder will undoubtedly result in success. Children often do try harder, and some make short-term improvement. In my experience, however, focusing on effort may even make a student's problems worse.

It would be easy, if you were the parent of any of the children above, to take the teacher's recommendations to heart. You might do what many other parents do: Give them a "You've got this" high-five. Express enthusiastic, non-specific praise such as "Great job!" when they do get something done. Offer to take them out for ice cream as an incentive. Tell them that if they get all of their work done this term, then you will buy them a new game controller. What have you tried? If you have tried any of these approaches, you are potentially missing underlying reasons for what seems like low effort.

For decades I have worked with people who are cognitively and sometimes emotionally different from what people think of as typical. We might imagine how much easier the lives of these people would be if they did not struggle against what others call the normal way of doing things. With a bit more effort they could be more like...not themselves!

Views of what's normal may be limited in many ways. For example, if you grew up in a household where the custom was to put on a sweater when you felt cold, you may think it strange that someone would talk about turning the heat up. If the custom in your household is to spend holidays together, you might chafe when a family member opts for a private trip instead. What do you think is the opposite of normal? Is it charming? Quirky? Weird? Wrong? Broken?

Identified or Actual Problem?

When students come to my office, it is usually not only because their grades have slipped, but also because they have apparently stopped trying to turn things around. It is the most commonly identified problem that teachers give and parents report to me. Often the actual problem is different from the identified problem. If you are a parent who just wants your child to get work over with, low or misplaced effort may seem like the actual problem to you. But your child's beliefs about learning and working independently can be the underlying problems.

What to Put in Place of the Effort Myth

I believe students would try differently if they knew how. This book encapsulates the primary lessons I have learned helping thousands of students find their own ways to successful learning. It includes helpful practices for parents to manage their own emotions and thoughts, to ask questions that support rather than judge, and to help their children learn skills, make choices, and build self-direction for moving toward success.

INKLING 1

Asking for Help and Not Getting It

One thing we all had to do more of during the COVID pandemic was be primped and primed for Zoom calls. One evening I was getting ready to host a live webinar. I was using someone else's account with more fun features than mine had. There would also be an unedited recording that would be published shortly after the presentation.

With an hour to spare, plus time for ten minutes of meditation and a final run-through, my checklist was all set. Login and password, lighting, sound, my presentation slides, clothes, hair, makeup, simple background, even fresh flowers; everything was ready. But then something about the username/password combination did not work. With just thirty minutes to go, I could not get onto the platform for the initial test.

I took a few long deep breaths, but I was feeling panicky. After trying to log in two more slightly different ways, I did what any teacher would say they want children to do: be a good self-advocate and reach out. There were call organizers and a tech coordinator. *Perfect,* I thought. *Someone can help!*

The Shame of Reaching Out

But I was wrong.

While I did receive a response by email, it said "Look it up," and "Everybody else figured it out."

That "everybody else" really stung. In my own thought storm I heard, *You are not as smart as they are. You have missed something obvious. It's not our responsibility to help you. Figure it out.* A follow-up soon arrived which was also unhelpful. It seemed to assume that I had not done the most basic things to help myself. It said, "Everything you need is in the attached document. You should have received and reviewed it last week." My question about the login, which could have been easily answered, was not there. In my mind, I heard their judgment:

Everybody. Everything. You should have. Figure it out.

Unfortunately, this is something that well-intentioned adults do to children all the time. We tell them to be self-advocates and to ask for what they need. A student is expected to:

- Know what they need

- Try to help themselves in a variety of ways

- Reach out as a final resort

- Repeat until done

When I reached out to get help, I opened a little window into what it must be like every day for many children. I can still remember the panicky feeling and the *never* voice that kept echoing in my head. My heart raced as I reread the direction sheet. My background thoughts boomed, *What obvious thing have I missed? Why can't I figure this out?* Then I coached myself out loud, "What's one thing you have not tried yet?"

But a louder voice, the one of anger and desperation, wanted to be heard, too.

Why won't you help me?

CHAPTER 2

Manage Life's Stormy Weather

To build the core parenting skills that prepare you to give the gifts of motivation, start with resilient thinking. It will help you to recognize the three parts of an emotion storm and discover how to calm the background noise that goes with emotional stormy weather. You can build skills for resilient coping, so that you know what to do both with sudden storms and when stormy weather doesn't seem to pass. Navigating toward realistic optimism will help you to avoid both unrealistic optimism and discouraging pessimism. Taking inventory of your child's resilience resources helps you establish opportunities for their growth.

You Are Safe Here in Stormy Weather

Have you ever been in an intense thunderstorm? It is loud, bright, windy, and wet. Now think of all of the terrible things that might happen in such a storm. Imagine trees down, power out, cars wrecked, streams overflowing, people harmed. Terrifying, isn't it? Or is it exhilarating?

"You are safe here." That's what my father said as we sat piled onto the tailgate of our old station wagon, garage door up, watching the lightning and tree branches whipping in the wind, and listening to the thunder and pouring rain. We all sat together watching the storm intensify and then pass. The warm air suddenly smelled delicious and clean. The clouds parted. The sun came out. There was even a rainbow.

"Isn't nature incredible?" my father said, obviously still in awe. Yes, it was. Though it was frightening in the moments of crashing and rumbling, we were all ok.

What if, instead, my father had said, "Lightning is dangerous. Get into the house. Stay away from the windows, and don't go near any water." What if he had never provided a safe place to survive and enjoy some of life's most spectacular stormy weather? While it is true that thunderstorms can be dangerous and that a person experiencing one may feel terrified, it is more useful and also true that you can learn to survive storms, actually feel safe, and even come to enjoy the intensity of the experience. This is also true of emotion storms.

When It Pours

We all get caught in stormy weather sometimes. Aside from the weather forecast, how can you tell when a storm is nearby? The atmosphere may feel heavy. You may even have trouble breathing, as if there is no air in the room. Then there is the thunder, the background noise of the squall that can indicate how close the storm is to you and how powerful it may be. When you pay attention to these signs, you can take shelter until the storm passes, just as we did in the garage sitting on the tailgate.

Stormy weather was my father's name for any kind of emotional outpouring that was stronger than the occasion called for.

The more you learn about the kind of stormy weather that is typical for your family, the more easily you can tell yourself a story about it that lets you take action intentionally and enables a quick emotional rebound after the storm has passed. When you get good at storm watching, you can even learn to rebound as the storm is happening. Building resilience starts with understanding the parts of an emotion storm:

Thoughts are the *thunder* of your stormy weather, your explanations, both aloud and to yourself, about problems. Your background noise rumbles because you tell yourself stories to make sense of stormy weather: What or who caused it? When will it calm down? What if things get worse?

Emotions are the *lightning* of your stormy weather, the feelings you have about the problem. They are the energy and intensity behind flashes of anger, fear, shame, sadness, guilt, and disgust. Emotions prepare you for action as the storm rolls on.

Actions are the *rainfall,* the automatic ways our brains and bodies are primed to act when our emotional stormy weather may drizzle or deluge.

The best place to start is with the thunder, replacing stormy thinking with resilient thinking. You can listen for background noise, hear the thought-story that is rumbling, and retell the story with also-true bits that may have been drowned out by emotional noise.

Changing a thought this way, even just a bit,
lets you take action more intentionally.

Slow Down the Process

When parents can slow down the wishing process and tap into their own and their child's thoughts, they can think through the gaps between a wish and the present reality. Resilient thinking depends on delaying decisions, even briefly, while you discover what is driving your thought process. This works for both children and parents. You (the parent) can take advantage of this extra time to plan with and not just for your child. Then you can plan more intentional action.

Listening for Background Noise: My Son's Guitar Lessons

When my son was in fifth grade, he wanted to take guitar lessons. I asked around and found a professional musician-teacher who was highly recommended by the school music staff and other parents. I bought my son a beginner's guitar. I found a time that worked for both the teacher and me. As you follow the rest of this story, notice the thoughts that made up my background noise, and the stories I told myself that led to unintentional action. As will be done throughout this book, background thoughts are shown in italics.

I am a good parent for nurturing my kid's musical interest.

The teacher seemed knowledgeable, organized, and professional. With high hopes and a declining bank balance, I wrote a check for the first semester's 15 lessons. My son was a complete beginner and would need lots of instruction.

This is a good plan. I am a good parent for sacrificing this time and money and for trusting the teacher's process.

The first lesson was only a little challenging. We arrived late and the teacher reminded me in front of my son that the time would not be made up at the end of any lesson, including this one. The teacher encouraged me to bring any concerns to him. He needed us to be prompt, he told my son and me, because he wanted to have all of the time scheduled to build skills that were my son's foundation for a lifetime of playing.

I am a responsible parent, and this won't happen again. I hope.

After the second lesson, the teacher asked how often and how long "we" were practicing. The truth was that "we" were not practicing at all, and it was my (mistaken) belief that the noise I had heard from his room was part of my son's expected practice. The teacher asked me to treat this like a homework responsibility, and to make a schedule and enforce it.

I'll try, but I'm not sure how to motivate him to practice.

By the third week, my ten-year-old son had decided that guitar was not for him. While he went to his room at the scheduled time, he refused to practice what the teacher assigned. The background noise of an approaching emotion storm rumbled.

Your teacher is expecting you to practice. We agreed that if you got a guitar, you would practice.

On the next lesson day, the guitar was nowhere to be found. Feeling flashes of anger, I decided that my son would have to tell the teacher that he could not find it. The natural consequence of a little embarrassment would help, right? I took him to the lesson, imagining that the guitar teacher must have seen other children who had lost instruments.

But the teacher had his own thought storm and said with some disgust, "People do not just lose guitars."

"I did," was my son's defiant reply, followed by an emotion storm of embarrassment and crying.

It is not supposed to be this hard.

I was now embarrassed as well as angry. I reminded my son that he needed to be responsible for his instrument and to his teacher, and I retold my thought story to him.

"Remember that you wanted to get a guitar and take lessons. You agreed to practice every day and take care of your instrument."

"No," he told me. "I said that I wanted to play guitar. You said that I would need to take lessons and practice to do that."

I had been excited that my son wanted to play an instrument. I imagined him happy and myself proud as he learned new skills to reach his dream of playing. I believed he would need lessons and assumed that he would both understand the need for and want explicit instruction. Could our student-parent-teacher emotional weather system have been managed better?

Anxiety is the result of fear that cannot be immediately comforted. Self-soothing skills developed through exposure to challenges can help people learn to manage anxiety. When we emotionally rescue children instead of asking questions that guide them to discovering their own answers, we may end up solving problems they do not actually have!

Think back to the beginning of this story when my son wished *to play* the guitar. At this point, I needed to slow the process down. Instead, in my own anxious excitement, I focused on solving my son's problem for him. I implemented plans before he understood the obstacles to making his wish come true. My adult interpretation, seen through the practical and somewhat prideful lens of parenting, was that my son's desire to play was a short-term opportunity to be grabbed or lost forever.

In contrast, here are my son's thoughts and wishes. To him, these felt true.

I wish I could play the guitar. I could have a band. We could be in videos.

It looks easy to learn. I could teach myself. A friend could teach me.

But I do not even have a guitar, and I cannot play. Maybe my parents will buy me one.

I just want to play the guitar.

Resilient Thinking is a Skill You Can Practice

Resilient people take steps to turn wishes into goals when the wish is meaningful, compelling, and makes sense to themselves. However, one of the fastest ways to *demotivate* a child is to turn their wish into required behaviors before they are ready. You may be unknowingly attempting to motivate them with a no-time-to-waste story. The more abstract their goal (being a guitar hero and video star), the harder it is to engage goal-driven steps and reach success. That's why long-term weekly lessons and daily practice might feel punishing instead of thrilling. The longer it takes to experience success, whatever that means to you and your child, the harder it is to stay motivated. The slow challenging slog to success will require both resilience and patience.

Resilient thinking is an ability to adjust to perceived crisis, challenge, and change. You do not need an emotion storm of natural disaster proportions to use it. Resilient thinking gives you the gift of time while you:

- Recognize that the emotional weather is stormy. Remember that it is temporary, even when it is intense.

- Notice thought stories that fuel the emotion storm. Know that other people could reasonably disagree with your point of view.

- Explore other also-true thoughts that calm the storm. Know that changing a thought gives you the power to change your action.

- Engage selective attention. Switch your focus to what is also true.

Managing Stormy Weather: The T-E-A Cycle

The two triangles in Figure 1 can help you manage the feelings that can turn into stormy weather by adjusting thought stories to ones that are also true and can help the emotion storm to pass. This is how to be a better stormy weather puddle-jumper.

Figure 1: TEA Cycles For Managing Stormy Weather

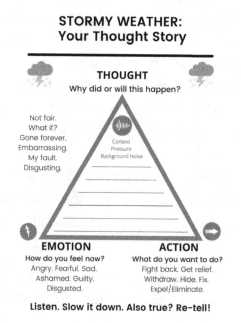

STORMY WEATHER:
Your Thought Story

THOUGHT
Why did or will this happen?

Not fair.
What if?
Gone forever.
Embarrassing.
My fault.
Disgusting.

Context
Pressure
Background Noise

EMOTION
How do you feel now?
Angry. Fearful. Sad.
Ashamed. Guilty.
Disgusted.

ACTION
What do you want to do?
Fight back. Get relief.
Withdraw. Hide. Fix.
Expel/Eliminate.

Listen. Slow it down. Also true? Re-tell!

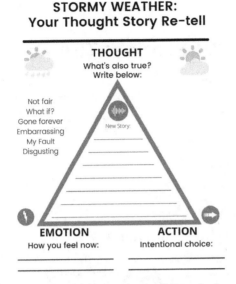

STORMY WEATHER:
Your Thought Story Re-tell

THOUGHT
What's also true?
Write below:

Not fair
What if?
Gone forever
Embarrassing
My Fault
Disgusting

New Story:

EMOTION
How you feel now:

ACTION
Intentional choice:

Listen. Slow it down. Also true? New plan!

Figure 2 shows the way the thought stories of my son, me, and the guitar teacher interacted. Everyone involved had thoughts and emotions. They also took action. My son used his unfairness thought, powered by anger, to make the guitar problem go away. My response to his action was embarrassment and anger, so I chose to make him tell the teacher about the missing guitar. The guitar teacher was angry at my son and also worried that he would not be able to do the job with an uncooperative child. You can see how everyone's emotion storm led to stormy weather all around.

Figure 2: Interlocking Thought Stories

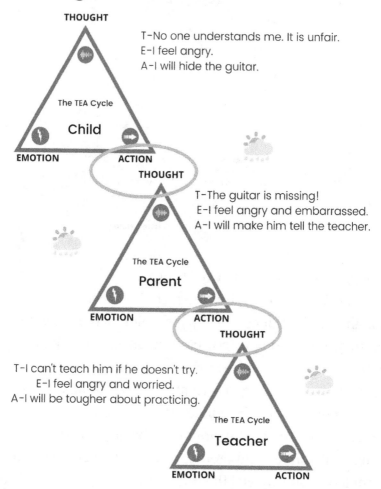

Thought Stories: TEA For Two+

THOUGHT

T–No one understands me. It is unfair.
E–I feel angry.
A–I will hide the guitar.

The TEA Cycle
Child

EMOTION   **ACTION**

THOUGHT

T–The guitar is missing!
E–I feel angry and embarrassed.
A–I will make him tell the teacher.

The TEA Cycle
Parent

EMOTION   **ACTION**

THOUGHT

T–I can't teach him if he doesn't try.
E–I feel angry and worried.
A–I will be tougher about practicing.

The TEA Cycle
Teacher

EMOTION   **ACTION**

That music teacher unknowingly encouraged anxious thoughts about what might never happen if action was not begun right away. The teacher communicated this with intensity. At the beginning the plan seemed like a good fit for me as a parent, but the music lessons were for a ten-year old, who at that point merely wished to play the guitar.

Resilient thinking is an essential skill for retelling thought stories that lead to stormy weather. Slowing down to tell a different story helps you stay in the game until you either reach your goal or choose a different path. You could use a set of blank TEA triangles like those in Figure 1 to analyze your own stormy weather and pick more resilient stories to tell yourself.

Sound and Music Success: Outcome of My Son's Guitar Story

My son went on to play five instruments including guitar. He played in a variety of bands for fun. He was a music major in college and worked in live theatre. As an adult he designed sound experiences for professional shows, working with playwrights and directors. As an audio engineer he tuned performance spaces for optimal sound and installed multimedia experiences in large retail and entertainment venues. There was no need for me to tell myself a never story about him.

When Stormy Weather is Part of the Climate: Elisa and Lucas

Sometimes the background noise in a family will be very loud, perhaps complicated by having multiple children and disagreements between parents. The stormy weather may be less like passing squalls and more like the climate.

Obi and Marissa had been married for nearly ten years when they adopted fraternal twins. Their marriage had been close but frustrating since they desperately wanted children and feared that they would be childless. They were very invested in not blaming each other for failing to become pregnant. A foundational thought story in their marriage had always been: "We are in this together." Until they weren't.

The couple were delighted to adopt infant twins. The children were very different right from the beginning. Lucas was quiet, happy, and easy to soothe. Elisa was active, moody, and could scream for hours. The pediatrician attributed this to colic that she would eventually outgrow, saying medically there was no cause for alarm.

By the age of two, Lucas chattered happily in sentences while Elisa spoke only a handful of words. Lucas held an adult's hand when they were in public together, while Elisa squirmed away. At the grocery store Elisa always got the seat of honor in the shopping cart with a seatbelt on, while Lucas walked calmly alongside his parent being a good helper. Elisa demanded treats and screamed when they did not go into the cart. Lucas learned to be a translator and peace-maker for his sibling. This was a valuable skill for managing the stormy weather in the family, which intensified as the twins grew older.

In school, Lucas fit in with his peers and developed solid skills, according to teachers. He had a good group of friends, enjoyed martial arts classes after school, and played soccer and basketball. Elisa struggled with reading, mastering math facts, writing letters, and sitting still. She was the first to spin in her ice-skating class, which she did even when it was not called for. Elisa loved writing graphic novels on her tablet using dictation. Instead of doing homework, she drew expressive anime characters for her stories.

While Elisa had many supports at school for literacy and math instruction well into middle school, the twins' parents regularly requested that they be in as many of the same classes as possible because it was the only way they could really know what was happening at school. Lucas readily shared his school experiences while Elisa mumbled when her parents asked about her day. If they pushed for more information, Elisa became either silent or enraged. Obi and Marissa had different views about what was happening.

"It's just not fair for Lucas to have to be the good one all the time," Obi complained to Marissa. "He needs to be his own person more."

"He's doing well in school and seems happy. Elisa is better behaved when she is with him. Why do you worry so much?" Marissa responded.

In some ways both parents were right. Lucas was a keen observer. He and Elisa had a genuinely close relationship that usually benefitted them both. Lucas understood that Elisa's challenges were not really his responsibility. He was a child, after all.

Marissa and Obi were often confused about the right thing to do. Elisa was a handful on so many levels.

Marissa found herself feeling lonely and without support. She wanted the family she had always envisioned before the twins, a recreation of the loving family that she grew up in. Her background noise chronically rumbled. *Elisa should do what she is told. She does not care how I feel. I deserve better. I wish someone would help. Obi doesn't care. Lucas is all I have.*

Obi withdrew from the family conflict. *It's never getting better. What were we thinking?* He spent more and more time working late. When he was home, he was frequently on his computer.

Lucas, meanwhile, had plenty of background thoughts building. *My job is to keep my parents calm and my family free from conflict. I need to make up for what Marissa lacks. I am lucky to be resourceful and confident. Elisa has many struggles and needs my help.* Elisa had become the identified patient, the person in her family with all of the problems. Lucas started to feel that he was not allowed to have any problems.

None of these thought stories was leading to resilience.

Being able to listen to background noise, and understanding how it is driving feelings and actions, cannot always reliably prevent the coming emotional stormy weather. Parents also need to predict stormy weather based on previous behaviors and have resources ready when they cannot stay out of the way of emotional storms. When there are family conflicts, one child's skill at peace-making should not turn that one into the emotional manager for everyone else.

When Storm Clouds Do Not Pass:

These steps can help you deal with stormy weather and know when more help is needed:

- Recognize that the emotional climate is stormy. Watch and listen for thunderous thoughts, flashing emotions, and their deluging actions.

- Notice thought stories that fuel the emotion storm. Know that in your family climate, thought stories are different for every person. Accept that everyone in the climate is not experiencing the weather in the same way.

- Explore other also-true thoughts that can calm the storminess. Remember that while you cannot change the weather, changing a thought gives you the power to change your own actions, especially when dealing with others.

- Engage selective attention and some acceptance of the situation. Practice compassionate listening, even if you do not think you want to change your mind. You are not entitled to be right, but you are entitled to your opinion.

- Seriously consider support through therapy or counseling when the emotional climate is chronically and intensely stormy.

Asking for Help: Resolution of the Elisa and Lucas Story

Marissa and Obi realized that they could not solve their problems by themselves. They asked me to help them find their way out of their family stormy weather. I helped them practice looking for what was also true about their challenging situation. As Marissa and Obi became more accepting and supportive of the different ways that they handled parenting challenges, Lucas was able to step away from being the primary peacekeeper. They sought art therapy for Elisa, who learned to appreciate her own creative ways of dealing with frustrating circumstances.

After high school Elisa went to a college for the arts where she thrived. She later became an art teacher in a school for children with language-learning disabilities. Lucas chose a gap year in which he lived, worked, and traveled internationally. After studying international relations, he became a foreign service officer and then a diplomat.

Take Stock of Your Child's Resilience Factors

We all can think of people who made it after escaping poverty, learning disability, abuse, or life-changing illness. They had imagination and a sense of purpose. They envisioned themselves beyond the external factors that held them back. They also regulated their emotion storms and learned from their challenging experiences.

Researchers believe that people need two kinds of resilience to manage the storms of life. One kind comes from *protective factors*, that is, people and systems external to a person. The other kind comes from *responsive factors*, that is, a person's own reactions to thoughts, emotions, and actions.

Some of the top factors that support a person's resilience are shown in Table 1. You could use this table to take stock of your child's resilience factors on a particular date. Check off the items that are solidly or abundantly present in your child's life. How can you make the most of these factors so that they grow in value? Where do you see room for improvement? Take notes about how the factors show up.

Revisit this form periodically to keep track of resilience factors that are developing and note where you see positive impacts.

Table 1: Resilience Factors

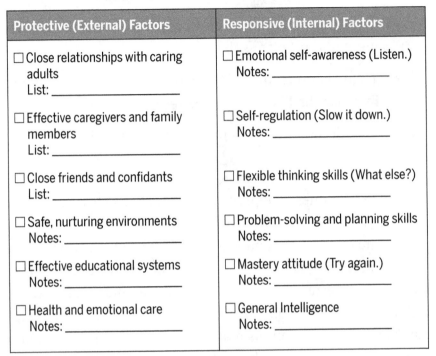

Protective (External) Factors	Responsive (Internal) Factors
☐ Close relationships with caring adults List: _____	☐ Emotional self-awareness (Listen.) Notes: _____
☐ Effective caregivers and family members List: _____	☐ Self-regulation (Slow it down.) Notes: _____
☐ Close friends and confidants List: _____	☐ Flexible thinking skills (What else?) Notes: _____
☐ Safe, nurturing environments Notes: _____	☐ Problem-solving and planning skills Notes: _____
☐ Effective educational systems Notes: _____	☐ Mastery attitude (Try again.) Notes: _____
☐ Health and emotional care Notes: _____	☐ General Intelligence Notes: _____

Appreciating and Managing Optimism

Some students, even those with learning challenges, are fortunate to have an abundance of optimism. As their skills improve, optimistic children learn that their developing strengths give them added control over school performance. Once they can reliably expect things to work out better in the future, these students are more willing to plan for and persist at challenging tasks. As a result, they can achieve greater school success over time, become less stressed, and treat disappointing performances as opportunities for purposeful improvement next time. Here are qualities that characterize optimists and encourage their willingness to keep trying in the face of challenges:

- They expect good outcomes in the future.

- Their positive expectations promote continued engagement and problem solving.

- Their continued engagement and problem solving increase the likelihood of better outcomes.

- Thus, their positive behaviors create a cycle of learning and growth.

But sometimes children are unrealistically optimistic. This happens when they can imagine achievement but do not yet have the skills and self-awareness to plan ways to get around potential barriers to success. They may have relied on the strength of raw memory to keep up with school learning before that ability alone was not enough. Two related symptoms of unrealistic optimism are deflecting blame and not taking action. They sound like this:

- "The teacher did not tell us."

- "It was not on the assignment list."

- "The assignment was not posted."

- "My lab partner did not answer my text."

Unrealistic optimists often blame other people and factors they think are outside of their control. Because they do not know for sure what else they could have done, they fail to take responsibility. They believe on some level that a poor performance might have been avoided, but it could not have been their fault.

Can students develop realistic optimism with thought patterns that are both positive and accurate? This topic will come up further in Chapter 8 on learning executive functions. It often takes added structure, including detailed planning steps, for student work to improve. Initially adult helpers can make the planning steps quite explicit, even requiring them in a certain sequence. As success occurs, some of these stepwise training wheels can come off, and the student can create more general learning plans with the help of an adult or peer.

Overcoming the Power of Pessimism

What about pessimists? Interestingly, they may or may not have good academic skills. In general, they do not imagine themselves being successful. Pessimists engage in negative self-talk. Their background noise tells them that things will probably go badly and that there is nothing that they can do to improve the situation. To avoid feeling even more disappointed in the future, they expect things to go badly. If things do go well or even somewhat better than expected, a pessimist may feel a combination of surprise and relief. These emotions can feel good, even if their actual performance is not. The pessimist's own behaviors will have had little impact on their success because they did not do anything more effortful or out of the ordinary. They may think:

- *I'm already as good as I can be.*

- *I'll probably fail.*

- *I'm not smart enough.*

- *It's not worth trying anything extra.*

As a result, it is more challenging to get them to experience their efforts as valuable.

Parents can help their pessimistic children by using specific praise that connects behaviors to actual results. You may need to use lots of positive evidence and specific examples to help your negative-leaning child learn to see their own effective behaviors at work.

If you are an achiever who likes to get things done, you may feel a strong urge to judge your child who seems not to be trying at school. Curb your instinct to correct and criticize. Avoid threats that paint a bleak future if your child does not turn it around.

CONCLUSION

Stormy emotional weather cannot be completely avoided, but managing it is nearly always possible. Resilient thinking gives you the gift of time. You can accept intense but temporary feelings, notice the thoughts in the stories you and your child are telling yourselves, change those thoughts even a little bit, and switch your focus to more productive thoughts that are also true.

INKLING 2

Discovering Myself Felt Like a Luxury

When I was twelve years old, my parents told me that I needed to get a job to learn the value of hard work. This was their response to my wishes for nicer clothes, a newer bike, and a family vacation involving boats. "You'll get those things by working for them," my parents told me. They even found me my first job, babysitting every day after school.

I imagined that a family vacation involving boats would be wonderful. By the time I was fifteen, I did get vacations with boats by being a nanny for families who had them. The first time this happened, the family's vacation lasted for a whole summer. I was not enthusiastic. My wish was for an enjoyable vacation, not a six-and-a-half-day work week that lasted for months! Housework, food and bathroom messes, child supervision every day? Yes. Weekends were worse. The seven bedrooms were filled with visitors whose beds needed making and towels needed washing.

I wrote letters home pleading for my parents to rescue me. Perhaps my summer situation seemed glamorous to them, but it was real work. I felt terribly homesick, but I could not return home until the end of the summer. I earned only a little at the time, but I learned a lot. In particular I discovered what now seems like a delicious irony. What job would I *never* want to do for a living? One that involved dealing with children and families.

That is why I smile when people who see my work today ask how I got my start. They assume that since I have been successful, I must have always wanted to be an educator, author, and consultant, and that I planned the career I now have. Instead, it was the result of many accidents.

I started college at age seventeen. Having left high school after just three years, I was a whole year ahead of schedule. Despite being academically very capable, in college I did not actively work towards building a transcript for a graduate or professional school. Instead, I listened to my background noise. *How will you pay for that?* was the loudest song booming on my internal playlist.

In college I double majored in history and English and minored in psychology. These were fun discussion-based classes where it was easy for me to find friends and figure out how to please professors. I took science classes for more of a challenge, and became a teaching assistant in the anatomy and physiology lab. I also tutored in the writing center, since it paid hourly rather than just a stipend, I worked off-campus as a waitress and a nanny, and took on odd jobs like house-sitting and cleaning. I was still dealing with children, families, and messes. Busy and organized, I was making no headway toward a profession.

"That's ok," my advisor said in the first years of college. "That's what you're here for: to discover yourself."

I thought of identity building as a luxury as unattainable as a cruise in the South Pacific on a private yacht. I was often on the edge of being broke after paying for rent, food, and my used car. However, my biggest fear was not destitution. I feared having to choose an unappealing real career and be stuck in it for 30 or 40 years. Pay the bills but be miserable? Not for me. I was already doing that.

CHAPTER 3

Be Your Child's Ally

In this chapter you will learn more about the ways that background noise affects the choices you make regarding positioning, seeking help, advocating for your child, and intervening on your child's behalf. We'll also explore the ways that managing your background noise helps you leave the door open for appropriate risk-taking by your adolescent and why that makes a positive difference for their future choices.

The Social Force of Positioning

Positioning. It is something we connect with marketing and product placement. If you are a parent of a teenager, you may have been creating the product version of your child ever since they were small. Maybe you have wanted them to have more opportunities than you did. Perhaps you imagined a scholarship for a top private school, elite team, or university.

In a data-driven world, you are regularly faced with high-stakes school testing that may make you wonder. *How does my child really measure up? How much more do I need to be doing to be sure that they are in the best possible position for success?* These questions can understandably lead to anxiety about your child's achievement, as well as confusion about how best to invest your resources in their education. You may also think, often without seeing any conflict, *I just want my kid to be happy.*

Social evidence seems to prove that positioning pays off. There are window decals. Swag. Social media. You may use these cues in your social environment to give you a frame of reference for what is valuable and within reach. When your child succeeds in school, social cues can generate relief and positive information that achievement goals are both worthwhile and possible. When you attend a school concert, art show, or athletic event, you may find yourself comparing your child to others with pride. But when your child struggles, you may have twinges of guilt and fear. *What if they are always behind? Am I doing everything I can for them?*

Be Your Child's Ally

It is so exciting to imagine your child filled with joy and focus while using their talents to become an expert at something you can be proud of, too. Can you separate that wish of yours from your child's wish, even for a few moments? You can, by being your child's ally. Here are some steps that help you become an ally. These are steps I learned to take with my son as I reflected on the guitar story described in the previous chapter.

- Explore your child's wish in order to understand what they really want without leaping to judgment or planning.

- Listen to your background noise. What thought story is it telling you about the need for speed?

- Go slowly. Breathe. Ask open-ended questions. Do not feel compelled to make their dream real for them too quickly.

- Manage your own expectations. Expect lots of ups and downs when children start lessons of any kind. Even the grittiest performers and athletes have times when they want to quit.

- Do not try to protect your child from failure. Stay rooted in the positive and expansive feelings that your child's dream offers. It is ok to be positively unrealistic in your imagination!

- Choose other allies for your child who support their wish and who do not unintentionally motivate with fear. I will say more about this in Chapter 5.

Positive Risk-Taking in Adolescents

Anxiety can be super valuable because it helps you respond to danger. While some problems can be scary, anxiety can help you make plans to prevent the scary thing from actually happening, or you can put a plan in place to manage the inevitable.

Anxiety can also feel like a delightful sense of exhilaration that encourages risk-taking. Positive risk-taking can build resilience at any age, and it is especially important for adolescents as they begin the deeper work of establishing their own identity within their peer group. Every parent will wonder at some point if a risk their child is taking is just too big.

Letting a Child Venture Forth: Kayli's Story

When Kayli was thirteen years old, she was invited to a friend's tiny cottage on a big lake. It was not a fancy place. It had a simple kitchen, bunk beds, an outdoor shower, and a campfire. All Kayli would need for her long weekend away would fit into a small day pack. There were no cell phone towers or devices there, just an old-fashioned payphone on a post along the dirt road that led to the small summer community.

Her mother's background noise rumbled. *I can't believe I'm going along with this.*

Before she got into her friend's car, Kayli's parents each reminded her about being responsible, wearing sunscreen, packing her first aid kit, minding her manners, and not going out too far into the lake because she was not a strong swimmer.

Her father's background noise rumbled. *I never did things like this when I was a kid.*

"Will there be boats?" they asked the friend's parents. "Please don't let Kayli go without a life jacket and an adult." With firm assurance that she would be safe, Kayli buckled up and her parents watched as the car drove off with their youngest child.

Both parents thought, *If anything happens to her, it will be our fault.*

Parents suffer from peer pressure, too. Kayli's parents did not want to look scared or overprotective of their middle school girl, so this time they let her go against what they felt was their better judgment. As the friend's car pulled away, they began to worry about Kayli and conjured a continuing collection of what ifs.

While they were pleased to see their daughter following through on a plan, something that was not typical for her, they could not let go of the possibility that something would go wrong. This was a new friend whose parents, while they seemed nice enough, were unknown to Kayli's family. They might be too lenient with Kayli, who could be impulsive. Or they might leave the girls unsupervised to do who-knew-what-with-whom. So many unknowns.

Kayli's parents believed the world was full of dangers. They also believed the world was full of things happening for reasons beyond human knowing. They believed they were careful and that other parents, maybe even those parents, were often careless. Any mishaps would reflect on their own irresponsibility and failure to protect Kayli.

There were many temptations at the lake, but on the first day Kayli only splashed close to the edge. In her background noise she heard her mother's voice reminding her that she was not a strong swimmer. The social scene, however, was out in the middle of the lake on a large platform dock with a swim ladder and cleats for tying up. Boats, that is. To get there you needed to swim or paddle or motor out.

Kayli's background noise rumbled something else. *Everyone is doing it.*

The next day a few more families arrived at the lake with their boats and their teenagers. Kayli's friend seemed to know everyone. The children had easy confidence with each other, both near and on the water. Kayli watched them with both great admiration and a bit of social anxiety. Though she had never even been in a boat before, it looked pretty easy. It also looked pretty safe since most of the children did not wear life jackets, except the ones on jet skis. That looked both terrifying and thrilling!

After lunch that second day, Kayli's host parents announced that they were going into a town about ten miles away to get a surprise for the girls. "Please don't go out to the platform dock while we are away," they requested. "Got it," Kayli's friend replied. This brought some relief to Kayli, whose parents had never left her alone except with a relative.

Later in the afternoon the sound of a creaky trailer announced the parents' return.

We are good parents for getting our girl her own boat, the friend's father thought to himself.

"It's small and easy to maneuver," the friend's father announced proudly. "I brought extra gas for the little engine. There are oars in case you run out of gas."

"You're always planning!" the mother teased. "No more than four people at a time, or she'll swamp," she cautioned the girls. Then she beamed proudly, "You're going to love it. Take these life jackets. Enjoy your new freedom!"

I wish my parents had done this for me when I was growing up, the girl's mother thought.

Kayli sat in the front of the boat as the girls set out to tie up at the platform in the lake. She felt that familiar sense of thrill and terror as her friend started up the motor. *How did she know how to do that?* Kayli loved the feeling of flying across the water.

"Here. You try it!" Kayli's friend offered. "I'll teach you." The little outboard motor came to an idle, and Kayli walked unsteadily to sit next to her friend in the stern to take the tiller. The lake was expansive and deep. The little boat soon moved smoothly across the water as it approached the floating dock.

Kayli suddenly panicked. Her friend grabbed the tiller and a crash was averted.

"Whoa! That was close," her friend laughed. "We live to tell!"

Unlike Kayli's parents who believed the world was alive with things beyond their control and that unfortunate outcomes were a bad reflection of their own risky parenting behaviors, Kayli's friend's parents believed people were in charge of much of what happened to them. They approached danger beliefs with optimism, as well as learning and safety behaviors. They saw the world as full of opportunities for excitement, sharing, and connection.

Parent Fears and Peer Pressure

Did you make predictions about how this story would unfold? People often take for granted that what they believe about the world is true and right. Are you open to challenging your beliefs? Thoughts and beliefs guide behaviors. Sometimes the truth that people hold is a function of background noise they never pause to hear.

Kayli's parents spent their weekend terrified that something would go wrong. They felt relief when their daughter arrived home safely. Kayli experienced both anxiety and exhilaration as she made new friends and learned new skills for operating a small boat safely.

You will also face parent peer pressure, passive and/or resistant children, things beyond your control, and teachers who have their own thought stories. Remember to listen to your background noise. Slow down the process. Consider what is also true. Re-tell your thought story. This is how to plan and act intentionally.

Creating Teacher Allies: My Story About a New School after a Move

When my children were both in grade school, our family made a big move. My new job was over an hour away from home. Each day was packed with commuting, program development, teaching, and additional responsibilities as assigned, even on weekends. Both children played town sports, participated in after-school classes and clubs, and worked at making new friends. Like many mothers, I was proudly sharing my own oxygen mask and waiting for someone to hand it back to me. I was too overwhelmed to be much good at asking for it.

I was trying to be the mother who could do it all for everyone. But I was slowly fading out, chronically sick, and my children were on strike. This was frustrating since their work looked so simple compared to the load I was shouldering. *Couldn't they just do it?* My background noise was more than a little embarrassing, considering my line of work.

Teachers sent home notes. For the older one, teachers described lack of focus and schoolwork that was unfinished or completely missing. Plus, she read books in class and during recess! Did I not realize that this kind of behavior predicted problems in middle school? Well, maybe that was my background noise.

For the younger one, they detailed careless work habits and irritability. He even told a teacher, "No!" when asked to demonstrate a math problem for the class. I was almost proud of him for knowing how to draw the line to prevent public failure, but the teacher was concerned. Did I not realize that he was not taking risks, an essential part of being a second-grader?

I was not even sure where to begin. That's because like most parents, I needed help separating my own background noise from what I was hearing from the teachers. Before I could help my children manage better at school, I needed to listen to my own thought storm. *What am I missing? It should not have to be so hard.*

I agreed to parent conferences. To make the meetings constructive, I knew I needed to stick to a script and stay away from any blaming or shaming.

Script for Parent-Teacher Conferences

The following prompts can be used to shape a constructive conversation with a teacher about what's going on in the classroom.

- **I notice**: Mention what you are observing and the conclusions you draw from it.

- **I feel**: These words show that your response is subjective and about your own emotions rather than a statement of fact.

- **I want**: Describe what you would like to see instead and what you are willing to do to help.

- **Will you...?** Ask for something specific that you feel will make things better.

In Table 2, you can see how I used these prompts and later documented one of my meetings with a teacher. You might do something similar for one of your meetings. Notice that there is a column for initial thoughts, which are often what NOT to say. In my case, I recognized that they were unlikely to make the situation better, since they could come across as judging the teacher rather being open to learning from them.

Table 2: Preparing to Talk to a Teacher

Initial thoughts. May be what not to say	Refined message to use in the meeting	Teacher response
I notice...there is not enough homework in your class. I can't tell if my child is learning anything in your class.	I notice that there does not seem to be much homework. My child says they do not have any homework most days.	Homework is assigned on Monday through Thursday each week. Some children finish the work in class or during reading period. The rest is to be completed at home.
I feel...I ought to know these things and it's not right that you keep parents out of the loop. I am worried that my child may not be telling the truth.	I feel ...confused about expectations ...worried that my child may be confused, too. ...unsure of my role from your point of view?	I list the homework on the board and on the classroom management system on Google. Parents can see what is expected there, but children should do their own work.
I want...you to be clearer about the way you assign work. I don't want my child to miss important things and then get a lower grade on something they could have done if you were better at organizing the assignments in the first place.	I want ...to be proactive and make sure that my child is not missing out on important learning. ...to know about struggles before they become big.	This is a great goal. We want students to access their own work both live and online. We think your child can do the work we assign independently but just needs to try harder.

Initial thoughts. May be what not to say	Refined message to use in the meeting	Teacher response
Will you...stop making my child struggle unnecessarily to learn content because the assignments are not straightforward? Stop burdening me and set things up so my child can do them successfully on their own.	Will you ...point me to your curriculum highlights for this term and your homework expectations for this week? ...list priority items that I can show my child? ...help me learn how to guide my child to the work you expect?	Certainly. We can check in more frequently with your child and encourage them to ask questions when confused. If assignments still aren't being handed in regularly, we can initiate a home-school communication plan.
...It shouldn't have to be this hard and they are trying. I'd rather not wait.	I am looking forward to increased communication from you. It sounds helpful. Let's start this week.	

I wanted the teachers to offer three things in writing, not just out loud, so that my children could be more independent and I could be more helpful at home:

1. **Weekly curriculum highlights.** Offer previews of coming attractions and weekly planning for learning and work expectations.

2. **Structure and focus.** Make sure my children can find and do their work. If my children aren't finding their work, break assignments down into more obvious sequential steps.

3. **An accountability system.** Let's have regular daily check-ins and communication until they are not needed.

Next time you have a parent-teacher conference about a difficulty you and your child are facing, try forming your own script with *I notice, I feel, I want, and Will you?*

Avoid the Instant Replay Loop

Maybe you feel you are in an instant replay loop with school. It can be hard to listen to teachers who tell you that this time will be different when your child may have struggled with similar issues in the past. For children and parents, each new school year and teacher tend to offer a new start. Sometimes that is exactly what you want and need. But some important information about how your child learns may not be promoted along with your child. While this may sound obvious, there is a critical difference between the way you view your child's difficulties and the way the teachers do. You have been watching your child for much longer.

If your child has struggled before and you have had similar solutions offered in the past, it can be easy to feel cynical about help. Your relationships with teachers form an essential foundation for advocating for your children. Of course, you are entitled to your thoughts and feelings, just like I was. But all actions, including different kinds of communication, are not equally helpful. What's more, when you want to be an effective advocate for your child, some asks will require a slow and often frustrating start. It is important to know what you want and not to confuse that with your emotional background noise. That's why I stuck to the script.

Take Your Power Back by Forgiving

Sometimes it can be helpful when you advocate for your child to do it from a place of empathy. Other times you may need to make space for deeper feelings before that can work. One way to dial down your emotions is to practice forgiveness for all of the slights of school years prior to this one.

Early in my career, before I had children of my own, a school psychologist put it to me this way when I complained to her about a demanding parent: "Everyone is doing the best they can at any given moment," she said. "When you focus on what someone is *not* doing, on how they are making *you* miserable, you are inviting *their* life in. Offer compassion, offer kindness, and do not give their negative thoughts power over you."

Forgiveness is not automatic. It is something that you choose. It happens in small stages. You give up your anger and negative judgment about the person who hurt you. Yes, it was unjust or thoughtless. However, *even* if you can no longer trust them, you can still forgive and maintain your boundaries.

Forgiveness is not the same as pretending that a wrong is right. It is understandably very challenging since you may need to give up the sense that you have been wronged or cheated. You aren't erasing the memory. You are taking its power away.

Why forgive? Because the sense of injury is a heavy weight to bear. Why remember? Because there may be patterns from year to year that are worth recognizing and learning more about. Only through the accumulated experience of being your child's parent will you know how to advocate for what is needed. But the judgment and fault-finding? They sap your power which you should never knowingly give away. Leave grudges behind. Let them go.

Knowing What You Need

Being a good self-advocate means asking for the help you need, but first you have to know what you need. If you have requested support from school and have come to believe that your child's challenges are more than lack of effort, it is completely normal to wonder if you should push for them to do something different versus just hanging in there. Who will have the solution if communicating directly with the teachers has not worked? How do you go about getting this help?

Just like Samira's parents in the story below, you may be faced with difficult choices about how to advocate for your child. Decisions about sharing diagnostic findings and seeking special education can feel very fraught when weighted down by the social fears in your background noise. How will you explain to your child why learning is harder for them than for their friends?

Trade-offs Concerning What You Need: Samira's Story

Samira had a history of language-based learning challenges. In her public school, children with certain types of diagnosed disabilities were placed in well-staffed but somewhat separate pull-out classrooms. To her mother, these classrooms came with unacceptable labels and limits. Samira's mother had all of her daughter's learning and psychological evaluations done privately and kept confidential. Even though services for developing the skills Samira needed were available at her school, her mother did not want her child to be educated with children that she thought of as disabled in one of "those" classrooms.

This was an interesting tradeoff. Samira struggled academically. Reading, listening, speaking, and writing were important in every subject, and she was not developing her abilities at a rate that kept up. On the other hand, Samira always had good friends and a positive life in her community where it was highly stigmatizing to be in the disability classes. By eighth grade Samira had barely survived academically, and she was recommended for the lowest level high school classes. This was going to mean that she and her friends would be going separate academic ways.

Samira's mother realized that this was partly her doing, but she did not want her daughter to be in the lowest level classes in high school for both social and academic reasons. She was an effective advocate for Samira, eventually getting her scheduled for the college prep curriculum. Samira also had plenty of after-school extra help on the calendar. She was able to see some of her friends, but her school anxiety escalated as ninth grade unfolded. The pressure was on for college-bound students to earn admission to prestigious schools. Academic expectations were high. Competition, real or imagined, felt crushing.

Academically Samira had some strengths in math problem solving, but she continued to struggle with reading and expressive language across all of her subjects, even with a tutor. Her mother continued to avoid school-based special education. From private evaluations conducted every few years, Samira had received diagnoses for Developmental Reading Disorder and ADHD/Inattentive type. Those words were never used at home, and Samira's mother hoped to keep these labels from her daughter.

Samira was told that she needed to work on fluency (smoother reading skills) and analysis that matched her social insights (comprehension). Samira discovered that with more customized structures such as graphic organizers for guiding the writing process in any subject area, she could express her ideas more clearly.

Since she had no other reasons, Samira attributed her struggles to not being as smart as her friends. She improved her self-advocacy by emailing directly to teachers about what she needed rather than just speaking with them. This way, Samira did not forget what they said, and she could look it up later by searching her email. It also benefitted her that her teachers saw her as *wanting to try*. For the most part they did not know what it took for her to be truly successful.

By the time Samira turned eighteen, she learned that her neuropsychological testing had yielded more than work suggestions. She had learning disabilities that were part of how she processed and understood the world both inside and outside of school. In some ways knowing that there were reasons was a relief. When she went to college, she qualified for accommodations such as extra time and a notetaker. It also meant that Samira started college with a solid work ethic but without the capacity to explain her needs to a future teacher.

Why didn't you tell me? Samira wondered. While she understood that her mother may have protected her from social stigma, she had lingering self-doubts and anxiety when it came to academic work. There was no way to know if her mother made the right choice in keeping Samira's diagnoses from her during her school years. The decision could not be undone. Not knowing meant she had no reasons for her difficulty besides the ones in her own imagination. Her mother had kept her from gaining the power of self-understanding.

Advocacy for Special Education

All US students are entitled to a *free appropriate public education* (FAPE). Special Education law requires this public education to happen in the *least restrictive environment* (LRE). It means being educated with peers in a general education classroom unless a student's disability prevents their learning needs from being met there. You've likely heard about *inclusion*, which is just one way that schools keep peer students with and without disabilities together in general education classes.

Special education is like going to a medical specialist. The classroom teacher is like a primary care provider (PCP). If all is well, the PCP is enough. If you have a problem that the PCP cannot address, you go for testing and are referred to a specialist. Or maybe not. Maybe your PCP concludes you have a compliance issue or need to make lifestyle changes. Oh, well, the PCP cannot be responsible for everything. Something similar may happen in schools with special education professionals.

Measuring Effective Progress

Nearly all students are expected to make what is called *effective progress* in general education classes. When this does not seem to be happening, trained special educators, aides, and specialists may work alongside regular teachers to support children who are struggling. If your child is struggling, and general education in-class supports are not working, you may wonder what can be done. School districts in different states deliver support in different ways. Often, a school may not be able to provide more help without your child going through a free formal evaluation process (testing) to determine eligibility for special education.

Some districts have excellent evaluators on staff, and others outsource this testing. If your child has never been professionally tested, and you have no known family history of learning, attention, and executive function challenges, you may be inclined to use your school district's testing. Free is good, right? It depends on what you want from the testing.

One of the most important things every parent should know before agreeing to testing by a school district is that it will not result in any diagnoses, even if the same testing done by outside paid evaluators would. That's because:

- Schools are looking only for the educational impact of a child's disabilities, particularly in the classroom, since that is what they are responsible for.

- School evaluators are not licensed by their states or held to the same standards that private evaluators are.

- School evaluations are not designed to be comprehensive. They usually focus on the suspected areas of disability and their impact at school.

Learning, attention, and executive function challenges generally have broader impacts than classroom performance. Private evaluations can be expensive, but having a diagnosis, much more in-depth testing, and expanded interpretation of the testing can be worth the cost. Even private evaluators can vary greatly in the types and amount of testing they do, the kinds of reporting and recommendations they offer, and the fees they charge. You can ask your pediatrician for referrals, inquire in your parent network, or search online for the kind of evaluator you need. If money is your decision-driver, know that some evaluators may work on a sliding fee scale and others take various insurance.

Being an Educated Consumer

When you begin the evaluation process for your child, there will likely be attempts to gain information from you first. School or private evaluators may interview you and require you to fill out questionnaires. To prepare, sort through your observations, thoughts, and feelings. Start by making a list of the struggles you have noticed and how they show up in your child's behavior. How long has this been a problem? Weeks? Months? Years? When did you first notice it? What have you tried at home that has worked? What do you believe might work, if only there was more of it? What interventions, if any, has the school tried so far? Have there been measurable positive results?

You are part of the individualized education program (IEP) or child study team. Since you are undoubtedly the person who cares the most, you will absolutely have to keep after the school to be sure that the plan that is formed is effectively implemented. This is not the same as micromanaging. Of course, the more you know about the actual responsibilities of school personnel, the better off you will be when it comes to asking the right person for what your child needs. In my experience your child will get the most out of working with school personnel when you are able to spot:

- What the system does well

- What individual people working in the system do well
- What is working for your child at school

CONCLUSION

Whether your child is found eligible for special services or not, you can learn to be their advocate by being open to their wishes, resisting peer pressure, letting them take appropriate risks, making sure that information about their learning needs follows them when they change teachers, and building an effective working relationship with school systems. All of these actions benefit from being aware of your own background noise and perhaps finding a more beneficial interpretation of what you are observing.

INKLING 3

My Temporary Career Beckons

By the time I was a college senior, I had some threads of my future story written, but I had no outline and the submission date was approaching.

"Try law school," the history professors offered.

"How about applying to med school?" the anatomy and physiology professor suggested.

Adults in my family helpfully reminded me to prepare for the leaner times that surely loomed ahead. "Get a job! Take whatever you can get. Don't take risks that involve money and debt."

No one suggested that I become a teacher, and I did not imagine my future in a classroom. "You are lucky to have work," the front-desk counselor at the college career center remarked. I was actually feeling worried and not-so-fortunate, but I sighed quietly and otherwise kept this to myself.

My background noise thundered away while she skimmed my resume. *It could not be! Did she mean that the assorted jobs I already had were the best I should expect?*

The career counseling protocol was that I should take some tests to determine my real interests and personality traits. No one, the counselor assured me, was interested in everything. "Answer this questionnaire. Don't overthink your answers. Respond as if you are in a work situation," she directed.

Which work? Bathroom scrubber? Dinner server? Cat cadaver coordinator?

The test results said I should be an artist. This was equal parts hilarious and horrifying. I came from a family with people who were real artists, ones who created visual art and music for a living. I did not believe I was one of them. I was good at singing, photographic composition, and sketching. I dabbled in calligraphy. I knitted, and I designed patterns for sewing tailored garments. I appreciated art. I was not, however, a *real* artist. There was no future story there. *Please, is there a different test?*

Another assessment asked me questions about my values. The results said I cared about things like these: Creativity. Improvising. Independence. Innovation. Flexibility. Helping.

In a serious, flat voice, the woman in the office said my best hope for a career should start with imagining what I would look like wearing a uniform. I had no idea what she was talking about, and the last thing I wanted to do was wear badly tailored work clothing that somebody with no fashion sense had chosen for me.

Of course, as she suggested, I could stay in school and work at my odd jobs, as if those were less appealing than being a management trainee at Burger King. This was her top recommendation. They would hire me full time, train me, pay my benefits, and just like that I'd have a career path that could weather a financial downturn. I would be working in a major corporation.

I was stunned and crushed. I had hoped the testing would help me discover myself. Instead, I felt sucked under an invisibility cloak. *Did she not care that I could learn almost anything I put my mind to? What about my ambition and willingness to work hard?* I could solve complex problems, teach people to write well-defended essays on topics I knew nothing about, and guide my students to learn the anatomy and physiology of animals preserved in formaldehyde.

"No," the counselor said, shaking her head. "Smart is not enough. You need a career that will mold you into a full-time worker for a company."

I knew that she was wrong in some important ways, but I did not know what would be right.

CHAPTER 4

Ask, Don't Tell

Coaching your child well is an important core parenting skill. It involves understanding the importance of providing a soft emotional landing so that your child wants to come to you with their concerns and wishes, even when you may not be able to solve their problems. It also involves asking lots of questions in a spirit of curious inquiry. Asking questions with a coaching mindset helps your child succeed. In particular, these questions do not imply that you are judging them and expecting failure. Coaches also use other strategies than the common parental practices of bribery and punishment.

Self-Advocacy at Home: Soft Landings

Whether you want your child to come to you immediately with questions or approach you only when they have tried on their own first, the solutions are similar.

The first thing to do is create emotional space for a soft landing. First, check in with your own background noise. If necessary, adjust it as described in Chapter 2. When I coach parents, they are often amazed at how much noise they carry around about their child being lazy, faking difficulties, and requiring so much energy.

Often when well-intentioned parents offer help, they convey an expectation of failure or a belief that the child is just not trying. Here's what children pick up, along with *what they might think in response:*

- "You'll never get to college if you do not work at it."
  Leave me alone. You don't get it. You think I'm stupid.

- "I struggled, too. I wish my parents had gotten me help like the help I have gotten you."
  I'm not like you. You're not living my life. I already have enough school.

- "Just do it. It's only for the rest of the year."
  A year? I said I don't want to. Stop nagging. No!

- "Why don't you just _____ ?".
  You don't get it. Maybe I'm just stupid.

We all have background noise on our personal playlists. Chronic worries and long-ago slights can emerge when we are stressed or triggered. Before you set about either jumping into or helping your child avoid the latest problem, try these steps.

1. Tune into your background noise and then adjust it by using a strategy such as mindfulness, reframing, breathing, or self-compassion that works for you.

2. Listen before you solve. It can be very simple and sound like this: "I'd like to help."

3. If you cannot help right now, make an appointment for the soonest time you can help, on the same day, and set the timer to stick with it. Keep your promise.

4. If your child has solved the problem themselves by then, great! Ask them to tell you how they approached the task. It is important for students to learn what strategies work for them and to say them out loud for both their own benefit and yours.

5. Keep track of these gems on a What Works list. The next time your child faces a challenge, they can consult their custom-made personalized list, and try a strategy while they are waiting for your help.

6. Do

   » Ask, "Can we review the directions together?"

   » Say, "When you did X, that was a solid first step. What do you think the next step could be? Good! Here's a sticky note. Can you write that down to help you remember?"

   » Praise their effort when they tell you what they did successfully.

7. Do not say, "See? You did not need my help," or point out what they should not do.

When you create a soft-landing space there is emotional safety so both you and your child can be more honest and vulnerable. Creating a soft landing pays dividends as they grow older, when you will want them to come to you with life problems that are even more challenging than school.

A Hard Landing: Sherri and the Cupcakes

When I was in elementary school, my family moved in the middle of the school year. Being the new child in a class that had been together since September was hard. There was a lot to learn about being part of a new community with different rules. In my old school we walked home for lunch every day. In this school there was hot lunch served in a cafeteria, with trays and steaming food, and a conveyor belt for the dishes and silverware.

In my old school, we celebrated birthdays by singing the birthday song. In my new school, children got to bring cupcakes on their birthdays. That year my real birthday was on a school day. I was thrilled when the teacher asked if I would like to bring cupcakes for the class. "Yes, yes, yes!" I imagined making the cupcakes myself and decorating them with chocolate frosting and sprinkles. They would taste delicious, and I would hand them out to each of my classmates with a smile. When I got home from school, I couldn't wait to tell my mother the good news.

"The teacher said I get to make cupcakes for my birthday and share them with the class. I told her I was putting chocolate frosting on them." I gushed with excitement. My mother's response was a hard landing.

"Don't you ever say 'Yes' to things like that. I don't have time to cook for other people's children today. I have enough to do already." Ouch. I did not even bother to say that I could try to make them myself.

I remembered this story when my own children came home with what seemed like impossible requests. Especially after we relocated several times, I understood why only a few weeks after a move my mother might have felt overwhelmed while managing three young children and trying to turn a house full of boxes into a home. As a child, though, this taught me to temper my enthusiasm and to be careful when asking for what I wanted.

Responding to Good News

Your response style to their sharing is also important when your children of any age bring good news home, even if it is not desirable from your own point of view. Here are the various ways you can respond to what the child considers good news. Only one creates a soft landing.

"That's great." You could say this and sound polite. You could also infuse it with sarcasm and communicate the opposite. Either way will effectively end the dialogue and make you seem uninterested in the conversation.

"That's great but..." or "That's too bad." These responses also make for hard landings. They are the set up for pointing out why the good news might actually be bad news, at least for you. This happens when your background noise is rumbling worry or unfairness alerts. You will sound critical and discouraging.

"That's one more thing I'll have to manage." Responding this way showed me that my good news was bad news for my mother. Even if it is true that you will be impacted, you will seem distracted and self-interested if you respond this way. Especially for younger children, this can be confusing. It can make it hard for them to know how to share or self-advocate if this seems to be a pattern of adult response.

"Tell me more about..." is a positive soft-landing alternative that allows you to keep the conversation going while you work through to a resolution, even if it is ultimately a compromise. This lets your child know that you are interested in them sharing with you, even if you cannot completely embrace their future plan. With less judgment and more curiosity, you open up the conversation so that more sharing occurs.

Soft Landings Build Self-Advocacy Skills

To create soft landings, remember to check in with your background noise first and then think about how you could respond to your child. Here is an example of a dialogue that could have happened between me and my mother that would have provided a soft landing.

Mother: "You sound excited. Tell me more about your idea."

Me: "Every kid gets to bring in cupcakes for their birthday. We have a party whenever someone has a birthday. For my birthday I want cupcakes with chocolate frosting."

Mother: "What is the time frame?"

Me: "I need them for tomorrow. My real birthday is a school day! I will have a party at school."

Mother: "What ingredients and materials would you need?"

Me: "Last week was Stefan's birthday, and he had cupcakes with vanilla frosting. His mother came to the party, too. She brought soda and little cups, plates, and napkins, just like a real party!"

Mother: "That sounds like fun for you. I will check my schedule. Can you see if we have the ingredients we would need?"

Me: "I will look. No, we don't have paper plates or cups. We have napkins. There is not a cake mix or frosting. We only have cookies in a box."

Mother: "What can we do with what we have so you can have a party at school tomorrow?"

After turning down your own background noise first, here is what you're doing to create a soft landing for your child:

- You are listening to them and willing to take the time to hear more, without judgment or direction.

- You are willing to collect more information about the context of your child's requests or challenges before reacting unilaterally.

- You show that you believe in their ability to manage disappointments, discover their own strengths to resolve conflicts, and move ahead with resilience.

- You are teaching your child that with your help (and eventually without it) they can:

  » Sort through their own feelings (excitement, worry, sadness, embarrassment...)

  » Understand the complexity of decisions and that not all wishes are possible

  » Choose solutions from available options, even when they are disappointing.

Asking Questions is the Key Skill of Coaching

For all children, but especially those with learning challenges, school responsibilities can be overwhelming. That's why your child may need a coach to deal with assignments that require more learning self-help, such as accessing online assignments and resources. How can you be that person? By learning how to ask, not tell.

Here are some of the skills you will need to draw upon to be an effective coach for your child when they are facing something that they feel is difficult:

- Ask yourself whether they have the skills that the current challenge requires. We will explore skills in Chapters 6 and 7, but the key idea for now is to assume that your child would be doing the work if they had the necessary skills and knew how to apply them.

- Ask what is also true. Listen to your background noise. Slow the process down. Calm the emotion storms for both of you. Wonder what your child needs or wishes.

- Look for barriers to success. In Chapters 8 and 9, we will explore what executive functions your child needs and how to help build them. At this point, you may need to add structure so your child can accomplish tasks, learn content, and improve skills.

- Observe your child's experience of this struggle. Uncover ways they are already using strengths and help them think of new ways to use the capabilities they already have. It is more motivating in the short term and more powerful in the long run than continually trying to fix what is wrong with them. Chapter 10 has more about recognizing strengths in action.

- Model what it means to be a learner. Teach your child to tame judgment of themselves and others. Let them see you addressing something that you do not already know how to do. Breathe: Slow it down. Listen before you solve. Figure out the next step. Reach out for help with a specific ask.

Blinded by the Situation: Theo's Story

Theo always did his homework at the kitchen table. While one of his parents made dinner, the other sat with him to be sure he was doing his homework. This began when he was in early elementary school. He struggled with reading and staying on track after a long day at school. His math facts just did not stick, even with lots of flashcards at home. His parents took turns working with him because it was exasperating to have to figure out how to help with homework after a long day at work.

Theo argued about what really needed to be done. "You weren't in my classroom today. You don't know what my teacher really wants. This is optional and that means I don't have to do it if I don't want to, and I don't."

When Theo was in 5th grade, his parents divorced. They had shared custody of Theo and his younger sister. The family home was sold, and the parents lived apart but in the same city. The children spent every other day and every other weekend with each parent. Theo's school difficulties were blamed on the big life transition that came with the divorce. His parents seemed to forget that he had always struggled.

His parents still worked with him at the kitchen table, but now Theo could add, "Mom/Dad doesn't make me do that," to his argument repertoire. He was using his social intelligence strength to distract his parents and amplify their background noise. His workspace at the kitchen table competed with meal-time space. Both parents tried to rush him along.

"Come on, slow-poke," his mother said. It was a gentle nudge, but it still hurt Theo, who was slow at many things: Reading. Taking tests. Handwriting. Typing. Getting the gist of directions in class.

"Hey, buddy," his father said. "How's today's world domination coming along?" It was meant to be funny, but Theo felt as if the world were crushing him, not the other way around.

Judgment Language

Theo's parents were using judgment language, even if you think their comments were gentle or funny. To be your child's coach, you first need to learn to ask questions without judgment and state the truth without foregone conclusions.

More obvious judgment language can sound like the examples below. Each statement is shown with the parent's background noise.

- Get your work finished because I need you to set the table. *Your slowness feels selfish to me. I have needs, too.*

- You should get your work done before dinner. *We never get to see shows together because you're still working. I feel like you don't even want to spend time with the rest of us.*

- I'm so done with your homework habits. *I did not sign on for this life. You're on your own.*

- Stop feeling sorry for yourself. *Where's the fight in you? You don't even try.*

I Knew It! A Turning Point in Theo's Story

One day it happened. By now Theo was in the eighth grade. On the portal page before each of his parents, separately of course, was proof that Theo was turning it around. They each felt that tingle of excitement. His mother sighed with relief. *Yes! Theo could be a high achiever.* It was a jump in his English Language Arts grade! But the happy thrill soon gave way to suspicion. *What led to this? Why now? What about all of those missed opportunities earlier in the year?* Each parent dove into the portal pages to get more details. There it was: an A on the most recent test.

I knew it, his dad told himself. *Taking away video games the day before the test was totally worth it.* He felt relief because he had wondered at the time if the punishment was a bit harsh. He began to feel angry. His background noise rumbled. *Why was it necessary to punish my child to do something he could obviously ace?* What do you imagine he said to Theo after school? It might have sounded like this:

"While you were at school, I went into the grades portal and saw that you got an A on the English test."

What came next? I have shown some common possibilities below including the ways they might backfire, as the remarks after the arrows indicate.

- "When you don't play video games, your school performance obviously improves. So, no more games except on Fridays after school." ► May create a conflict around something that Theo wants

- "You should be proud of yourself, Theo. Look what happens when you apply yourself." ► Tells Theo what to do and how to feel, taking away opportunities for Theo to build self-awareness

- "Great job! You are smart and have so much potential. We are going to track your grades on a chart and I'll study with you on a regular basis." ▶ Swoops in to save Theo, thus reinforcing his belief that he cannot succeed alone

- "Listen, we can go for ice cream at your favorite place, just as soon as you're done with your study guide." ▶ Bribes Theo instead of letting a natural reward work

- "Let's call and tell your mother." ▶ Shows Theo off, rather than having him share what went well with pride

Until this fine showing on a test, Theo's parents were likely either to send implicit threats, "Even more video games will be withheld," or charge in to protect him, "Let me see that essay." Both approaches suggested that they were worried and that failure would mean discipline. They were conveying to Theo that they needed to protect him from this expected negative future. But he was more likely to be worried that they were worried about his potential, which seemed to hang precariously in the balance.

What Could Theo's Parents Do Differently?

First, his father could check in with his background noise, noticing that he was jumping to conclusions about the cause of Theo's performance. After all, he would need to run his own clean research study to know with certainty that Theo's English test performance was more than loosely related to removing video games. It is far more likely that this particular test was a better than usual match for Theo's abilities. Even if negative emotion such as fear or anger were part of the recipe, it is not sustainable for either Theo or his parents to rely on jumpstarting him that way. Moreover, his parents did not really want Theo to be miserable in order to perform successfully.

His father could try asking Theo what went well at school. If Theo shares that he got an A on the English test, his father could ask, "What was good about that?"

Theo might say, "My grade went up."

His father could respond with another question. "Cool. How'd you study?" At that point, Dad would need to watch his line of questioning. This is not a cross-examination but instead a way to get Theo to think about what positive things he did that contributed to what went well.

Building Confidence

A person's confidence is built through resilience opportunities, some guided and some that occur by accident, along with self-reflection. One of the best ways to practice this is to focus on what is working or did work well even in a challenging situation. It doesn't even need to be about schoolwork. Potential is unknowable. When you tie your child's future value to their performance on school tasks, you may be denying them the joy of small wins. These accumulated tiny moments of joy, and not the big achievements in life, are what build your child's sense of self and the happiness you really wish for them. One way to show others that you care is by asking what went well *every* day, not just after a big test!

What about the school portal? You can still check it. However, I'd recommend that you do it weekly or less often, around the same day and time. That is one way to keep from being overly focused on grades.

But what about challenges, you ask? Use the same "Tell Me More" response you learned earlier in this chapter. In my experience, this approach works to help people talk through a challenge as well as to share a win.

When you can listen to your child without judgment, and with compassionate curiosity even when you want to swoop in and save them, you facilitate a conversation rather than a potentially impulsive solution delivered with anxiety or anger.

Replacing Unhelpful Go-To Strategies with a Coaching Approach

It is a good idea to evaluate honestly the go-to strategies you use to manage your child's effort. The three P's shown below are commonly used approaches that can sometimes be marginally effective in the short term but are not helpful in the long term. As you look at these approaches, consider which ones come most naturally to you. What do they look like in your situation?

- Prevention: (Motivated by fear they will fail)

  » Do homework with your child

  » Send notes to the teacher to save your child from perceived failure

- Punishment: (Motivated by anger that they break the rules)

> » Confiscation: Take away tablet, games, social opportunities
>
> » Detention: Cannot leave workspace until assignments are completed

- Permission: (Motivated by shame and pity for them)

> » Give your child a mental health day, that is, a chance to stay home from school
>
> » Let your child sleep in and go into school late

I recommend using a coaching approach instead. A coaching approach is based on respect for your child's own learning needs and desires. One of the key skills of the coaching approach is to ask many questions without telling what to do. The sections below will help you create questions that you could ask to help your child do what needs to be done right now as well as build skills for facing future challenges.

Ask Permission Before Coaching

Before getting started with any coaching engagement, even one with your own child, ask for permission. You may think this is silly since it is your own child, but it makes all the difference for a student to believe that they have a voice in the process and some ideas to offer. You are letting them express their own feelings, wishes, and needs, if only briefly. I figured this out in the guitar lessons story in Chapter 2.

Your child wants to know you are listening to them and willing to take the time to hear more. When you ask non-judgmental questions, they may be able, with your help, to sort through their own feelings and solutions. This is often the only way to find out. You can collect more information about the context of your child's challenge and help them to discover their own strengths to resolve conflicts and move ahead.

Coaching Goals

Your goals as a coaching parent are to help your child:

- Understand and remember new information

- Connect new information to old

- Apply what they have learned in new ways

- Manage their time and energy to plan and complete assignments

- Work quickly and accurately

- Build resilience, self-regulation, and self-awareness

Coaching Questions

I have listed many questions in Table 3 that might be helpful at various points in your coaching relationship with your child. Get started. Go slowly. Remember: You are not asking all of the questions at once. Pick one or two to try and see what happens. Ask the questions with a spirit of inquiry and curiosity. Remember you do not already know the answers.

Table 3: Coaching Questions

Purpose	Questions
Open the discussion and ask student permission	• What was your day like? That sounds _____ (Affirm/Do not fix). • What is your work like for today? • How can I help? • Where would you like to start?
Discover student objectives	• What do you want to accomplish? • Where are the written directions? • What do you think is necessary to get this work done? • Where are the materials you need?
Uncover student strengths	• What is one thing you could do? • How is this like an earlier assignment? • What do you think has worked so far? (Make note, but make no judgment.)
Inquire about needs	• What is something you haven't tried yet? • Who else might have the information? • Who are the people that you can rely on? • Who has made you feel understood, supported, or encouraged? • What can you do until they get back in touch?
Construct time-wise plan	• What is your time estimate for this work? • What is the first thing you could do to make that happen? • What is the best place to begin?
Take measurable skilled action	• What skills helped the most on tasks like this in the past? • What skills are needed? • How will you know you are on the right track? • How did you advocate for yourself?
Reflect: Evaluate success	• What went well? • What have you learned? • What would you do the same way another time? • What might you do differently? Why?

Avoid Interrogating

Please do not treat this like a script where you need to ask all of the questions. Start small, and always ask permission first. As you discover what is working, systematically add complexity. When a student has not mastered the basics, adding expectations without actionable strategies just creates anxiety.

If you do not go slowly, children seeking reassurance or clarification about what is required may feel subjected to a full-scale interrogation. The adult, who may just want to know where to begin, may seem to be delivering a barrage: "How have you tried to help yourself? Have you looked this up? Did you ask a peer? Did you check the portal? Did you reread the directions?"

Be sensitive that it can be extremely difficult for a student with an accumulated sense of failure to separate questions that could help them succeed from the feeling that they are being judged.

That's why it is important to think of asking questions as if you were on a calm fact-finding mission. Children are very sensitive to judging and will not share with you if they think you will use the information to call them out later. Be sure to record your own questions and the experiences you have with them. As you practice you will have moments when the coaching question perfectly matches the needs of the moment. You'll want to remember!

It can take a lot of patience to ask instead of tell. The payoff can be a more trusting and open relationship with a more independent child.

Extending Coaching Beyond Homework

Here are some helpful hints for extending your parent coaching beyond homework:

- Engage: Try out your best questions, the ones you keep track of, for topics other than school assignments. Make "Tell me more" a normal part of every conversation.

- Admit it when you do not know something: If either of you are confused about ideas, look them up *with* your child. They can do the looking and the reading, as appropriate.

- Help your child use look-it-up tools for all sorts of words and information. Ask, don't tell means that if your child has a question for you, don't just tell them the answer; put extensions in the browser tray and use cell phone apps so they are readily available. (PowerThesaurus for Chrome or cell phone is my favorite for learning vocabulary.) Ask your child what they use in school.

- Record: Keep track of learning approaches that work so they can be recycled in real life. Ask a coaching question when your child feels stuck.

- Reward: Learning is its own reward. Specific praise that makes the child feel seen can help. Rather than "Great job!" "You're awesome!" "Way to go!" "You're so smart!" say, "I like the way you _____" with specifics about the actions that led to success. This is nearly always more effective than giving general praise.

- For Tweens: Make your coaching structured and dependable with fun and creative learning risks. Give choices that are acceptable to you. Be mindful of the language you use to describe challenges with tweens. Learning is not an enemy. Do not be like Theo's dad who talked about world domination. Do not use language like "killing it," "putting up a good fight," or "conquering" assignments or assessments.

- For Adolescents: Make your coaching structured and edgy without acting like you are too cool. Know your boundaries in advance. Discuss but do not bargain with older children. In bargaining, parents generally end up in the weaker position with a relentless teen or college student who has much more independence skin in the game than you do.

Theo Off to College

Theo left public school after eighth grade to attend a small parochial school where he became a three-season athlete. He was professionally tested and found to have a language-based learning disability and auditory processing disorder. These were things that his parents could not address alone at their respective kitchen tables. A combination of home support, school accommodations, and tutoring did help. He qualified for extra time on standardized and in-school testing, graduated with honors, and took a gap year before heading off to college.

A Word About Incentives

You may think it is useful to incentivize learning. To understand why that is not generally so, imagine that you have been offered more pay at work to do a new job that takes longer than your old job. Also, you do not feel particularly good at it. In the short term you might be happier with the pay increase. But if you did not feel supported and you were being evaluated based on your new work, you might soon be unhappy.

Yes, learning *takes* work. But that is not the same as thinking that learning *is* work. Paying children for grades dulls their curiosity. They may use their strategic thinking skills to do the least amount possible to earn the incentive. In my private practice I see this with rubrics. Some students are willing to target the box for an ok job so they can spend less time on their work. They have been incentivized to be good enough when they could be excellent. When this happens, their goal is not learning but just getting the job done.

Conclusion

As your child's coach, you can ask them questions to reveal what they already know and can do. You can share in the joy of your child's successes and be proud of their growth. Using coaching questions will help you to turn down your own anger and worry. This way your child can know you are listening and ready to hear more. They may be able, with your help, to sort through their own feelings and find their own solutions. Ultimately, you can collect more information about the context of your child's challenge and help them to discover their own strengths that will help them resolve conflicts and move ahead.

INKLING 4

Why Don't They Just _____?

Staying in school when you are good at being a student can be the path of least resistance. To save money, I chose a program that paid for my tuition, starting work on a master's degree in education. I had found myself a temporary career. I really enjoyed the course work: Tests and Measurements. Adolescent and Developmental Psychology. Philosophy of Education. Secondary School Teaching Methods. Missing from the required course list was Special Education. Supposedly I would not need it in general school teaching. The career center had a list of available positions now that I was tethered to a career path.

I was hired to work in a summer program for fourteen- to eighteen-year-old students from disadvantaged backgrounds. I had to sign a contract, so it felt real. I was barely older than the students, who had all failed school in some way that had gotten them referred to this program. From my point of view, they also had a shocking lack of school skills and work ethic. *Why don't they just _____?*

I could have filled in that blank with an endless litany of competencies they did not seem to have. Here were apparently intelligent children spending a summer at a camp whose admission criteria involved being a failure at the things that all children were supposed to be able to do. It seemed outrageous. Who had let this happen? It could not just be that they hadn't tried hard enough. How could this problem be solved?

My contracted job was to teach them biology, but nearly all of them had only elementary reading skills, so they could not read the high school textbooks that were provided. "Figure it out," the program director said. "That's what you're here for." He was not a teacher.

This was before personal computers or the Internet, so the children were without the benefit of YouTube, voice typing, or text-to-speech technology. In retrospect this did not matter since they really needed to do science in order to understand it. I created a hands-on walk in the woods to teach them a plant science curriculum that I cobbled together from the provided books. I also spent weekends at the library learning about learning, something that the graduate school teaching curriculum had left out. Could I teach the children to be smarter? This fascinating question drove my work that summer.

I dove into modifying the materials I had. I wrote simplified guided notes for my students with blanks for vocabulary, places for sketching, and pockets for collecting. I offered individualized reviews with oral testing. Students tested each other. We collected and mounted specimens. Many of the children had barely legible handwriting, so they dictated and I wrote the labels. I had them present their discoveries to each other. I could see small bits of progress. The children smiled more easily. They complained less.

At the end I had to write a page-long report about each student, explaining their before and after status. While I knew that my students had more biology knowledge, they did not have significantly better student skills such as reading, writing, math computation, and problem solving. "That," remarked the director, "is for the next teacher to figure out."

....

CHAPTER 5

Gather Allies

We have already explored what it means to be your child's ally in Chapter 3 and coach in Chapter 4. You do not need to be the only one. You and your child both need allies. In this chapter, you'll learn about different kinds of allies, including which are true allies and which are adversaries in disguise. You'll also learn how to spot allies among teachers, coaches, and other adults who know how to motivate your child to keep trying more effectively. They spot what is working. They offer appropriate praise and opportunities to practice. Chapter 11 will return to the topic of allies to explore the allies your child collects themselves, especially mentors and friends.

Parents Need Allies

One of the most difficult things to imagine before you have children is how much becoming a parent changes your life. Completely might not be an understatement. Before I had children, I saw parents with screaming toddlers in the grocery store and imagined with great certainty that this could never happen to me. I felt sorry for those embarrassed parents, but I also judged them. *Why don't they just...?* I'd ask myself, as if the struggle could be resolved with a little more know-how, discipline, or patience.

My first child was a non-sleeper. Just a few minutes of dozing off in the car on the way to the grocery store in the afternoon meant she could then be awake for most of the night. A quick doze in the car on the way to daycare and like magic, she was ready to face the day. I, on the other hand, was perpetually exhausted and sometimes short on top-of-mind strategies. That child also shrieked. Grocery shopping with her meant subjecting other shoppers to our toddler drama. What was I thinking that she could not have those sugar-coated cereal puffs? What possessed me to replace them on the store shelf she had secretly grabbed from? "She's killing me, she's killing me!" My tiny two-year-old daughter's piercing voice made other shoppers stare or quickly move away from us.

Have you ever *lost* a child in a public place? One of mine wrestled away from my grasp in a crowded store screaming, "Let me go, let me go!" Then she was gone. Total strangers will help when they think your child may be in danger. Another child was the hero of that scene, a boy a bit older than my then five-year-old. He asked if we had looked inside the round rack where pants hung tightly together. That is where he would hide if he escaped. There she was, very quietly singing songs from the *Little Mermaid* to herself, being Ariel in a theater-in-the-round of hanging pants. Thinking of this now makes me smile. She grew up to be a singer and very creative. But in my moment of terror, I felt like an angry, embarrassed failure of a parent.

Five Types of Allies

Until I had children of my own, I envisioned having heroic amounts of creativity, patience, perspective, and a never-ending good sense of humor. Of course, this mythical image of a real-life parent had flaws. In particular, I did not know how easy it could be to hear the antagonistic voice of judgment, *I ought to be able to do this myself* and its defensive counterpart, *But I did nothing wrong!* It turned out that I needed other people in my life to help me raise my children. I needed people who could size up a situation and understand what was needed.

Whether they knew how to act in an emergency or stuck by me during a period of chronic challenge, the following five types of allies shared their gifts of knowledge, empathy, and affection. Understanding the unique motivating gift of each type of ally can help you to spot them when they are present in your life or the life of your child.

- **Parents:** Love and support even when it is difficult. These can be your own parents or other people who know you well and have relevant experience.

- **Teachers:** Design effective learning experiences for your child and involve you when necessary.

- **Sports Coaches**: Uncover hidden possibilities that you couldn't bring out in your children yourself.

- **Mentors:** Help your child connect possibility to purpose. We will explore this type of ally in Chapter 11.

- **Friends:** Share honest affectionate companionship. Your own friends can be a terrific support. We will explore the friends your child makes in Chapter 11.

Parent Allies

When my children were young, I was fortunate to know a lot about child development and learning theory. I thought I was well-educated and experienced when it came to children. I was even married to someone who had good credentials for working with children. But no one knows everything!

Even if you think you are right about something child-related, it feels good to have your ideas affirmed. If you are ever even a little unsure about something, another person's input, especially when it bypasses you and is delivered directly to your adolescent, can be helpful. In the event that you are angered or baffled, another person may have an answer that you have not thought of yet. They may know someone else who can help. Alternatively, they may have no idea, just like you. Now you know this really is a tough problem.

Every child, especially one who has had learning struggles, needs parent allies who can love and support them even when it is difficult. A fortunate child has other people besides their own parents who look beyond challenges and see a completely lovable person presently trying their best, even if it is not looking good to adults. This role does not require being an actual parent.

Imagine this ally as someone who has as much heart as you do, but who does not have as much skin in the game. When a parent ally steps in, they will not feel intrusive to you. They will ask before assuming that you need their advice. You will be able to trust them because they are full of care without judgment.

It can feel both miraculous and infuriating to have your older child listen to what you think is the same message coming from another ally. *Didn't I just say that?* you may think, but must not say. You might even personalize this and imagine that you and your child are in an epic battle for gaining back control of your life. Parent allies who you trust and are not merely double agents for you are extremely important to adolescents. Imagine these allies having super-powers reserved for your child, without being their actual parents.

Why would you want someone else to be a parent ally for your child? Because a wise parent recognizes that sometimes they are too close to their own situation to be able to counter future fear with present opportunity. During challenging moments, parents sometimes slip and become adversaries. Instead of reaching only inward for resources, having someone who can mirror your parent role reduces your risk for disputes and burnout. It frees you to focus more energy on building a loving relationship with your child.

Beware the Parent Adversary

Some people are adversaries, not allies, in your parent story. These people push you to ask for their insights even if you do not feel you need or want them. Your close family members may think helping means criticizing the way you handle parenting. Your child may have grandparents who want to be very hands on, almost as if they are raising the child. They may give advice that seems like tests of loyalty. When they appear to embrace your child's interests against you, they can seem more like double agents than allies. Give yourself permission to stand your ground.

Teacher Allies

It is often said that a parent is their child's first teacher. You surely showed delight in your child's development and introduced new challenges so that your young child could learn even more. You noticed what worked for them and personalized it. You gave them a foundation for language, communication, movement, self-regulation, and social skills. You also noticed when things were not quite right with your child, observing them and experimenting with possible solutions, despite likely having little or no training as a teacher. By the time your child went to school, you already knew a good deal about how they liked to learn.

Teacher allies are master instructors who understand how learning happens for your child. They can design effective learning experiences for students who struggle. In ways that are responsive to the student in the present situation, they design learning experiences and take responsibility for teaching the way the student learns.

Teacher allies may not be officially teachers, and the most important lessons they impart may not be academic ones.

Special Cases of Teacher Allies

Sometimes the best teacher allies have other roles, even ones outside of a school setting. What they have in common is that they know what your struggling child needs, academically as well as emotionally. While having one of these roles below does not necessarily make a person an ally, this list can help you look for people who can meet special needs.

- **Special educator:** Addresses learning, attention, and executive function challenges that affect learning the curriculum

- **Speech-language pathologist:** Evaluates and treats struggles with language and practical social skills that affect intelligibility, written language, comprehension, and communication

- **Occupational therapist:** Evaluates and creates treatment plans for handwriting, visual organization, motor skills, or integrating sensory systems that affect planning, movement, stamina, or producing work

- **School psychologist or counselor:** Teaches therapeutic strategies for handling complex personal/social situations like bullying or anxiety triggers that create barriers to school and life success

- **Pediatrician:** Uses medical knowledge to manage struggles with self-regulation, especially when it affects physical well-being, attention, impulsivity, and school performance

- **Private therapist, coach, tutor:** Helps outside of the school environment where they are free to form coaching alliances with children who may struggle to trust or benefit from school-based providers

- **Theater director, art/music/dance/acting instructor:** Makes space for children to express themselves creatively and participate in effective group collaboration.

Sports Coach Allies

For many children, sports are the avenue not just to playing a sport, but also to developing physical coordination, learning the value of regulations, and discovering the camaraderie of working on a team. Sports can also be a welcome respite for children who struggle with other aspects of life. Some children seem to be natural athletes, quickly picking up new sports. Some thrive on team pursuits such as baseball, lacrosse, soccer, basketball, football, or hockey. Others may gravitate toward more individual sports such as running, track, swimming, golf, ice-skating, gymnastics, horseback riding, karate, or cycling.

The best sports coach allies ask questions even when it seems that telling would be more efficient. They are open to learning what specific children need, and they refine practices to meet specific needs. A coach ally can be an important part of a player's success, especially when a child has hustle but maybe not natural ability.

Not all sports coaches are allies. Youth sport coaches may have experience playing and coaching their sport, but they are usually volunteers with no professional training for working with youth. They may be focused on spotting the players with the most potential for winning. At the beginning of a season the potential for winning can seem exciting. But other children, including those with even mild learning, attention, and executive function challenges, may feel that their potential for more skilled play is overlooked.

When Winning Competes with Playing

There are competing reasons for playing any sport. For instance, a child may need to stay on a current team to be eligible to join a more desirable team later. Figuring out what is wrong when your child complains about a sports program can be complicated because there are many possible reasons why an otherwise competent athlete would choose to resist playing. How your child thinks about something can powerfully drive how they feel about doing it. For some, it can be challenging to keep trying when they feel as if other children were given a playbook in a language they do not understand.

Resilience in sports is tricky because a person needs to take at least some risks to develop more flexible thinking about challenges. By middle school, some sports programs are already extremely competitive, most children are not rewarded for just loving to play, and the number of chances to take risks that could build resilience often shrinks. As children get older, winning becomes increasingly important.

Sports Coaches Aren't Always Allies: My Son Strikes Out

Some sports coaches see weak players instead of ones who are still developing. My son played soccer. One year another player tripped him accidentally, causing my son to fall and break his arm. It was on the first day of tryouts, so he was out for the season. The next season, he was relatively out of practice, so he was put on what other children called a baby team with other less skilled children. They had a losing season, and he did not try out again. My son wanted to play hockey, but he was light for his age, making him a risk for injuries even with the best equipment. He was allowed to practice but benched for games. He did not stick with practice. He tried lacrosse, but by early middle school, children were already being sent to exclusive camps and being scouted for travel teams. The coach did not recommend him, and he aged out of youth play.

When he played Little League, my son's team wore the uniform of a major league baseball franchise that had ended up in last place in the previous season. Members of other teams called them losers. The coach did not hide his disgust when children whiffed or dropped a fly ball that it seemed angels had almost placed in their glove. My son was the last batter for the final Little League game of the season, and he struck out. Some spectators booed, and some parents called him out as he walked through the congratulatory hand-slap line, wiping away tears. It was his last baseball game.

How to Spot a True Sport Coach Ally

A sport coach ally understands how important it is to structure practice to develop success. These adults can be tough and have high expectations, and they also can build skills, structure practice for success, and give children belief in realistic future improvement. Here are some of the ways to spot a sports coach who can be a true ally for your child:

- They structure practice for developing success.

- During practice or play, they tell a child what to do, not what not to do.

- During practice, they do more than talk. They work players through the motions while describing what to do.

- They call out praise-worthy behaviors of all athletes, not just ones with top skills.

- They notice and praise growth out loud by describing how children are becoming more successful.

- They help children reflect on what they have done well.

- They help children understand how to incorporate specific measurable bits of practice the next time they play.

- When you as a parent ask how to follow up at home, they praise your child in front of you and tell you what to do.

- They make sure that everyone on the team plays at least some of every game.

CONCLUSION

You need allies who can help you manage difficult times, spot what is normal and good about your child's development, and keep things in perspective. Sometimes you need to assess whether someone is a true ally or is instead undermining your parenting. When children are younger, you may be very involved in finding allies and nourishing their relationships. When your child is older, they will start finding their own allies. We will return in Chapter 11 to explore the types of allies that your adolescents tend to find without your help.

INKLING 5

Student Teacher Success?

I stuck with my stay-in-school plan to become a teacher and was eventually placed in a large public high school for my teaching practicum. My students were 150 of the lowest level eleventh grade students in this school's United States history classes. At first, I had a mentor teacher, but she became seriously ill a few weeks into the semester, so I was on my own. I was too busy to be terrified. My advisor made me write lesson plans for each day, covering at least a week at a time. Ugh! No flexibility. But soon he stopped checking in.

Many of my students slept in class or cut class altogether. I wanted to wake them up and check in with them, but the rules were explicit about that: Do not do it. They did not turn in homework? Give them zeroes. They failed tests? Record the grades. The history department chair reminded me it was not my job to manage their home life, do their homework, or take their tests for them. If they weren't going to try, they were going to fail, and it was my job to give them the grades they deserved.

But I wanted them to be successful. *Why didn't they just _____?*

Were they just bored? Or were these students' school skills really not adequate for them to do the work the curriculum demanded? I knew what to do. Get them busy! Create something new! I did not wait for permission. It was late April and the mentor teacher was permanently unavailable; I would not be there forever, so I just did it.

"Imagine it is 1933," I told the students. "You have the chance to repeal Prohibition. Prohibition made it illegal to produce, import, transport, and sell alcoholic beverages throughout the country. There are good reasons for and against it. Should we repeal this amendment to the United States Constitution?"

The drinking age at the time was eighteen, so it was pretty easy to get most of these children to care that a constitutional amendment had made liquor illegal throughout the country. Could it happen again? For part of that week my class was like improv. Students drew facts from a hat and had to determine whether their fact was a reason to keep or repeal Prohibition. They worked in loose teams and developed special interest groups. A librarian helped students with the basic research. It was only for a week.

On the last day we moved the desks from their rows and turned the classroom into a makeshift stage. Students shared research and debated what would be good about Prohibition and what was actually bad about it. There was audience participation, and it was a little chaotic. But just about everyone was engaged. Students who were not on stage could even yell out suggestions for either side. Real learning was happening.

I learned something real, too. I had just failed my student teaching.

While my triumph of student participation was occurring, the college's student teacher advisor had dropped in unannounced. At the end of class, he called me aside and gave me the news that I would very likely not pass my semester-long practicum. "This was not teaching," he told me in no uncertain terms. "Students cannot learn in such chaos." I think he used the word "travesty" and wore a shaming "What were you thinking?" expression. I would not be progressing to the next step toward teacher certification. My temporary career was already reaching the end of its shelf-life.

I was able to get the advisor to agree to a return visit, but he told me that I would have to be a real teacher when he came back. This would also be unannounced. It all felt ridiculously threatening and unfair. *Creativity. Improvising. Independence. Innovation. Flexibility. Helping. What about those?*

What did a real teacher do? Stand in front of the class with notes, lecture from material in the book, occasionally write special points on the board, prompt children to take notes, and then provide written tests to discover what students had learned.

My advisor made me this offer: If I passed the real teaching test by doing those things, I could pass student teaching, but with the very lowest possible grade. However, my advisor would not write me a letter of recommendation.

Several years later when I was a teacher, I requested my administrative file from the college. Toward the bottom of the pile of documents there was a letter to the department chair, written by my advisor. He noted that I had "no future in the profession," that I was "on my own path," that I was "leaning toward insubordination," and "encouraging poor learning habits" in my students. Perhaps I had the career counselor to thank. The letter had never been sent.

PART 2

....

The Three Gifts

*It's not how hard you try: it's **how** you try hard.*

Now that you've explored the core basic parenting skills for building resilience, enhancing your coaching style, and becoming an ally, it is time to turn attention to the three gifts that enhance motivation by helping children try effectively.

The First Gift

When you give the gift of **Competence**, you make sure that your child has the solid basic skills for achieving results that they can care about.

The Second Gift

When you give the gift of **Choices**, you provide ways to offer some learning autonomy for your child so that results of their work are because of things they can choose and change.

The Third Gift

When you give the gift of **Self-direction**, your child can experience pride and accomplishment for its own sake, using the strengths, relationships, and self-beliefs that ready them for successful transition to college or directly to the world of work.

Each gift has two chapters that help you understand how to use your core parenting skills to offer the corresponding gift to your child. The first chapter gives basics, while the second chapter gives more advanced applications.

CHAPTER 6

Build Skills for Academic Learning

Succeeding in school requires a variety of basic and more advanced skills. You can help your child learn by detecting missing skills, personalizing learning recipes, and removing barriers. It is also important to understand the difference between strategies to build skills and accommodations that help children learn content before they have built skills.

Basic Academic Skills

Academic skills are the most basic requirements for our school learning. They are the four R's: Reading. WRiting. ARithmetic. Reasoning. These skills are not synonymous with ability or intelligence. Even highly intelligent children with exceptional language, visual-spatial, and motor skills can take a long time to learn how to read, write, and do accurate math calculation. Some may need a highly personalized program to build missing skills.

Why Your Child Needs Skills

Skills are processes and concepts that your child builds as a scaffold for learning information and solving problems. Reading skills (decoding, fluency, and comprehension) affect every subject including math. Once students are past learning to read, the expectation is that they can read to learn across the curriculum. When they can add, subtract, multiply and divide, they are expected to compute fractions, decimals, and percentages, solve problems with proportions and algebra, and manipulate formulas, especially for STEM learning.

Your child can have high intelligence yet struggle mightily to stay motivated when their skills develop unevenly. Those with low-average reasoning skills who also have strong memory skills may perform many school tasks satisfactorily, if without distinction, well into high school.

Many parents wonder if their child has skills on grade level. Grade level is a useful fiction about being able to do the work in a particular school or classroom but will not help you know where challenges lie.

The first thing for you to consider when your child seems like they're not putting forth necessary effort is this: Does my child really have the skills needed to learn?

Table 4: The General Skills that Every Child Needs

SKILL	EXAMPLES
Reading	Identification of real words, decoding for unknown words, comprehending main ideas and details
Writing	Communicating with language, using conventions of grammar and organization with a writing implement or keyboard
Arithmetic	Knowing math facts for adding, subtracting, multiplying, and dividing
Reasoning	Understanding what's being presented in language or non-verbal content; Applying skills for solving problems, including in math and science, to get an answer that makes sense
Selective Attention	Directing attention and focusing on what is important in any task and knowing where to apply the skills they do have
Following Directions	Being able to break down a large task into smaller steps
Fluency	Being able to use needed skills with automaticity and ease
Executive Functions	Being able to launch and manage the skills of mental and emotional self-control (These are discussed in detail in Chapter 8.)

What Does it Mean to Be Average?

It can be very misleading to hear that your child is average in school. It can cover up the real reasons for struggles with skills and motivation.

Do you remember the average, also called the mean, that you learned to compute in school? Add up all of the values, then divide by the number of values. Imagine your child had the five test scores 75, 82, 93, 62, and 85. Add them up and divide by five to get the average score, 79.4. It is a way of spreading out the damage of the lows and taking advantage of the health of the highs. That's an average test performance: 79.4 is C+.

Remember the excitement of Theo's parents when he had a high test score in Chapter 4? The 93 in the above set of scores indicates your child is not really average, right? Well, no, since this kind of measurement does not tell you if your child has the skills to perform better consistently. These scores have a personal range, in this case 31, the difference between 93 and 62. It is the spread between the high and the low for your child on what may be very different kinds of tests on different kinds of material, even if covered in the same course.

A score like that C+ compares your child's performance to a maximum number of points to be earned, not to a scientifically normed population of other students performing on the same test items under scientifically controlled conditions. With teacher-made tests, it means your student earned 79.4% of possible points that could be earned. That's all it means.

This earning of points can be affected by many things, including how students were primed to practice for the types of problems they would face. A teacher-made test is *not* about being in the average range of students your child's age. It is a curriculum-based test which will *require* skills like the 4 R's, but it does not *measure* them.

A different use of the word average comes from the way psychologists and educators talk about the normal distribution on standardized tests in a large population. They usually try to make the numbers easier to understand by using percentiles: having a score at the 50% percentile means a person scored better than 50% of people who took the test. Because percentiles are spread over 100, the results of standardized tests look the same as scores earned on classroom tests, but they are different.

The normal distribution or spread of the data is used to identify the *average range* of a large sample. You have likely seen it represented as a bell-shaped curve with the mean as the high point. This shows that performance on standardized tests exists as a wide range of normal, spread out so that normal is bunched up in the middle. Many things about us are measured this way, so it can be helpful to think about other standardized measurements.

Figure 3: The Normal Curve Showing the Average Range

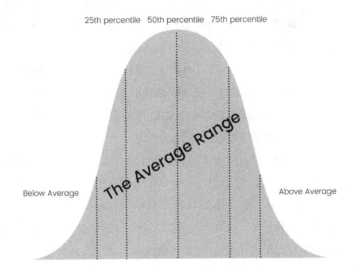

In a doctor's appointment, they routinely check your blood pressure. Is it normal relative to the overall population? More importantly, is it normal *for you*? Maybe you've been anxious lately and your numbers are up. Your scores can be compared to the range of all people who have their blood pressure taken as well as to your own test values over time.

Thinking about what is within the normal range can help us to identify what is developing well. It can also help us notice potential problems and outliers.

What Do Grades Measure?

In education the most regular measurement that children and their families receive is graded work and accumulated grades on report cards. You might believe that acceptable grades can be equated with development of learning. If your child mostly does their work and has enough school skills for studying and test-taking, there may seem to be little reason for concern if grades are your measure of learning. Grades are cues from the environment of school. Importantly, they are about performance, not mastery learning. The tests we use to track school progress and skills acquisition are not the same as the kinds we use to determine skills application.

In the age of standards-based learning with high-stakes tests given at each grade level in nearly every state in the United States, it is difficult to know if a student is truly learning specific skills. That's because the results of this kind of testing are a lagging measure, sometimes arriving four to six months after the tests are given. If your child is in the *needs-improvement zone*, critical time has been lost while waiting for those scores. Meanwhile, the report card may only say that the teacher believes that with more effort, more reading just the right books, or drilling math facts daily, your child's skills will improve. When this does happen, it may be with a different teacher altogether.

When to Seek Help

It is much easier to see that school struggles come from lack of skills when a child is in elementary school rather than in later grades because people tend to assume skills are already present in older children. When your child does not yet have solid academic skills and is struggling to learn them, it makes sense to explore why and opt for early intervention. But a wait-and-see approach is far more common among educators and even among professionals like pediatricians, since there is such a wide range of what is considered normal development. There are also gender and racial biases about expected behavior. Adults, even professionals, may differ broadly in their interpretations of what they observe.

When should a parent begin to explore the possibility that school struggles are more than a dot in the developmental range of childhood skills? If you have a family history of learning, attention, or executive function challenges, at this point you might wonder if your child has them, too. If this seems to be a new possibility for you, though, you may actually begin your search for helping your child by coming up with reasons why they do NOT have a diagnosable challenge.

You may think, *Why choose to discover a diagnosis of a learning, attention, or executive function challenge when more effort could be the answer?* You may end up trying many things before considering testing that might uncover something even more complicated than what looks like laziness. As a result, your child may struggle quite a bit before you are ready to begin the discovery process.

When School Support Hides What's Missing: Kai's Story

In second grade, when most of her classmates were reading at least some books to themselves, Kai tricked her friends and teachers into thinking she could read. During read-aloud time, she sat next to the teacher where she could see the colorful illustrations on each page of the book. The teacher was a very dramatic reader, and Kai watched her mouth and expressions carefully so as not to miss a single word.

Learning with a teacher who was trained in the whole-language reading approach used in her school, Kai used her fine oral language abilities and social insights to develop adequate but irregular skills. She was taught to use the context and make likely guesses. Kai stumbled through reading material, pretending to know words that she could not read in isolation. The teacher or a more skilled classmate offered gentle hints or corrections, and Kai moved along to third grade with emerging but spotty reading and spelling skills.

At home, Kai avoided doing homework that involved reading. By fourth grade, this included math problems and social studies. There weren't many pictures in the books anymore. But she could use videos to learn content and had discovered that if she pointed to a word she did not know, someone else would often read the whole sentence to her. This was a win since she was a champ at remembering what she heard.

Kai spent long nights at the kitchen table with her older sister who was a year ahead in school. Her sister was a great help. Until middle school, she told Kai what she needed to know to do homework and how to survive tests and quizzes. Eventually her older sister had plenty of work to do herself for school and could not help as much. While Kai's writing skills and test-taking were unreliable, the teachers had rubrics, check lists, study guides, and online practice tests. These reduced the amount of actual reading required. Kai survived middle school.

In high school, the school district evaluated Kai for special education services at the request of her parents and determined that she'd benefit from some accommodations, but she did not qualify for special services. Kai's reading decoding scores were then at the 25th percentile. Yes, this was technically in the average range. But in the context of many other exceptionally well-developed language skills, they were impoverished.

Instead of special services, the school said that Kai needed to take general level classes, try harder, and actually attempt the homework she was being given. They said she could not reasonably expect to learn how to read and write better if she did not actually try to read at home. Kai could also come after school for extra help one day a week for each class. This was a scheduling challenge since Kai was a three-season athlete, but she figured it out.

You may wonder how Kai made it to college. She discovered in high school that her teachers were much more willing to support her when she showed up for those extra help sessions. She used the social-emotional skill of "Make the teacher think you care." By getting to know the teachers and showing interest in their classes, Kai noticed that they dropped obvious hints about what was going to be on quizzes and tests. It was like what her sister had done years earlier, but it came right from the source! These insider trading tips supported Kai's practical goal of less reading, while she continued to learn content. In English and History, Kai received extra support for organizing essays. She did all of the extra credit and test corrections, often with direct teacher support.

Kai even won a school-wide award for her highly creative project illustrating healthy behaviors for teens. When she was a high school senior, teachers wrote glowing recommendation letters about her character and drive. Kai chose colleges that were test optional, since she could not finish the Critical Reading portion of the SAT under regular time constraints, and she did not qualify for extended time.

Kai's decoding skills were barely in the average range. They were not enough for her to be successful in college, even though the achievement test called them adequate by high school standards. Those weak decoding skills affected every college class except math. They also rendered it almost impossible for Kai to read and remember the multi-syllable anatomy and physiology words that made up a significant portion of what she was supposed to be learning in her nursing program. One particular textbook Kai was required to read was about 900 pages long and had no pictures, diagrams, or graphic information, despite being all about disorders and injuries of the human body that needed to be visualized.

Kai and I used a game I developed so she could learn a reliable no-guessing process for decoding. I also inquired about her notetaking and study approaches. She diligently searched the Internet for each word, listened to it being spoken, and repeated it aloud. She drew detailed, color-coded, and labeled diagrams for every vocabulary word and had put them on hundreds of flashcards. I asked her, "Have you been to office hours? Did the teacher have suggestions?"

The instructor had told her to just try harder to memorize the content, and that drawing was an obsessive task. He did not know that she lacked the most basic skill for learning all of those vocabulary words. Importantly, he missed that the illustration process was essential to her learning. It might not have been his way to learn, but it certainly was Kai's.

Once she could read any word, Kai used her skills to draw and label integrated cartoon-like diagrams that linked anatomy and systems. She was basically illustrating and labeling her own textbook while simultaneously learning to read accurately and learn the human body.

What Success Can Look Like: Kai's Story Turns Around

Kai went on to become an operating room nurse where her outstanding ability to visualize the human body in three dimensions was essential to her surgical team. Her listening and social observation skills, coupled with great willingness to accept and apply regular feedback, made her a sought-after professional colleague.

Learn to Taste What's Missing

While nearly all children will take comprehensive tests that identify their proficiency at accessing the curriculum, most will never take standardized norm-referenced test batteries of skills like Kai did. When PK-12 students are not referred for special education evaluation or private neuropsychological or other specialized testing, parents may accept report card grades and teacher comments as true measurements of their child's skills and capability.

Skills, particularly the 4 R's, are the basic ingredients of learning. Part of the magic of school, when it is working well, is that the ingredients for learning are structured into recipes, that is, the curriculum. In the early grades, skilled teachers mix and cook up learning lessons whose ingredients are focused on skill development. At this level parents are typically invited to help with the cooking. They are welcome to participate in children's learning directly, especially for reading and math.

What can you reasonably expect from basic ingredients? I'm sure that I do not have to tell you that a meal from a fast-food chain is not the same as one from a five-star restaurant. Fast food comes from a scaled system where a consistent but not personalized product is expected. While you might be able to customize your order in some fast-food restaurants with extras or leaving some things out, the underlying food components and choices are the same. If this was all that you knew, you might think it was normal to eat this way.

For some people, knowing what you are getting is part of the appeal. Huge corporate empires have been built on the value proposition of uniform quality, relative speed, and affordability. You probably wouldn't leave a fast-food restaurant saying that you had had a peak dining experience. What could make the experience better? Is it the food itself or the way it is prepared? What kind of bread? Do you want sauce with that? Given choices, it is easy to start imagining what might be missing. But without an ingredient list and some options, you may take what is on offer without imagining what would improve the nutritional value.

School is like that. There are many ingredients. Some can be customized. But to make that work, it helps to be able to taste what's missing. Fluency? Reading? Math? Reasoning?

Fluency: Processing Ease

Did you study a foreign language in school? Maybe you found the skill of learning new vocabulary and grammar easy, and you eventually mastered it. Maybe you even became fluent in more than one language. Fluency means that you can think, comprehend, and communicate accurately and efficiently in the target language. When you have the skill of fluency you are not constantly switching and translating back-and-forth from your native language.

Being able to call on learned skills efficiently and use them as needed is also called fluency. Skills fluency means this same kind of automatic recall and application. Your child may be struggling with skills fluency if they find a task like reading or math effortful. In upper grades, fluency challenges can affect every subject area.

If this is your first or only child, you might have nothing to compare your child's struggles to except your own school experience. Trouble with accuracy during oral reading and for-getting math facts when problem solving might be your first indication that something is missing. If those skills seem to be developing, even if it is slow-going, underlying struggles might still be overlooked. By the time a child reaches middle school, the expectation is that their skills foundation is adequate, if not secure.

When your child is *dysfluent*, you may have the feeling that they would be more accurate if they went more slowly. The speed-accuracy mismatch can show up in struggles with reading comprehension, following directions, retrieving math facts, and copying, just to name a few. Fluency is also affected by abilities such as processing speed, working memory, and switching. Chapter 8 covers the importance of switching to learning.

There are many possible reasons for a student to be dys-fluent in one or more skills. Sometimes it is a matter of them needing direct teaching of what is missing. The student needs it served up to them. Other times dysfluency is connected more broadly to processing speed issues.

This book is not intended to teach you how to diagnose the underlying causes of problems. Instead, you should know that if your child struggles to read smoothly and accurately, with appropriate expression and phrasing, this will affect their understanding and enjoyment of written material. If they struggle to retrieve math facts, they will find doing math work, especially solving problems, frustrating. Chronic challenges like this wear away at motivation.

It is not enough to memorize facts, whether for language, math, or other content areas. A student needs to be able to retrieve the right ones at the right time for the right task with efficiency.

To improve reading fluency, teachers recommend that chil-dren increase familiarity by reading more. Yes, the number of exposures to a word does tend to predict learning the word. This makes sense, since you cannot get better at something by not-trying. Remember, though, that success is not about how hard you try but *how* you try hard. If your child reads the target word wrong each time or skips it entirely, multiple exposures will lead to multiple miscues. Over time, multiple miscues affect comprehension and reasoning.

Think of Kai. She learned to memorize books by using rhythm and rhyme as well as pictures. She got people to read enough to her that she did not miss out on most content learning. She took advantage of test corrections and retakes, and her teachers were won over by her work ethic. This was her dependable recipe for grades, but not for reading decoding. Until her teacher supports disappeared in college, Kai survived. But she knew that the reading was not making sense. Many other students will disengage and call the work boring or stupid.

My entire career has been about creating personalized learning recipes for students who struggle. They do not want the work to be so hard and to feel less-than for not being able to figure out how to do better.

I believe that the vast majority of learners would try something new if they only knew how or what to try. Your child with fluency challenges can benefit from lots of relatively easy-to-implement learning strategies if you explore new ways to look at their challenges, stop judging them for not trying harder, and support them with real-life patterns.

Reading: Perceiving Practical Patterns

Trying harder with more opportunities does not automatically mean a student will learn missing skills. Students also need to understand patterns. Patterns are repeated elements in the natural and abstract world that when noticed can make learning, connecting, and recalling information more efficient. Some patterns are remarkably simple, but they may be invisible to a student until someone shows them.

Students may turn out to be quite skilled at finding patterns once they have been revealed. For example, a child might notice that words beginning with un- make the base word have the opposite meaning. Happy becomes unhappy. This might make them curious to learn about other word parts and their effects on base words. For instance, why is "unresponsible" not a word? Younger children who are still learning grammar and usage may overgeneralize patterns like this. If overgeneralizing any rules persists into later grade school so that students struggle to be more flexible in their thinking, they may find it hard to get unstuck from rules. This can impact learning.

Some students rely on memorizing without understanding. This can make it look like they are mastering math because they can recite facts. On a test, though, they might struggle to apply those facts to solve problems. They might be able to memorize high frequency words but fail to notice the patterns for dividing longer unfamiliar words. For someone like Kai who had solid language and listening but not decoding skills, learning patterns such as the seven kinds of syllables and five ways to divide them was life-changing and gave her access to her chosen career. Even a person with dyslexia and related language and listening challenges learns to read this way, albeit with supplementary direct teaching of additional specific skills.

Comprehension: Expecting Things to Make Sense

When my children were growing up, we often read aloud after dinner. It helped that we choose books that were age-appropriate, high interest, and that encouraged repetition. Early readers and younger elementary students often love books that are silly or that rhyme. As your child becomes more sophisticated, there are many other types of reading to try: news, poetry, humor, fiction, non-fiction, graphic novels, and mystery are all appropriate.

You can share reading this way with your children for free or at very low cost. We visited yard sales where books were cheap and the library where they were free, and we used the content that came home from public school. Teachers often have a class library of well-loved books and can make suggestions. We swapped with friends and took advantage of inexpensive media mail rates with friends who were not close by.

What about reading on a device? As a parent, I learned about my children's interests and kept track of their skills development by reading with them. When they misunderstood, missed patterns, or needed more explanation during these shared reading times, I asked questions. While reading on a device can give independence, a wonderful goal, keep in mind that when your struggling child uses assistive technology, you may miss out on moments of language and concept development, connection, and fun. Keep reading with them yourself.

Teach your child the skill of reasoning. Do they understand what has been read? Are they connecting to other relevant information or just memorizing? It is essential that learners use reasoning skills to know when to stop in a reading selection, whether in a print or digital book, and that they know how to get more information when something does not make sense. When they read aloud, you get a window into their thinking. This is priceless! When you send them off to use an audiobook, you cannot keep the audiobook track from just moving along. But they can learn to stop the recording intentionally with your guidance.

Find times to listen with your child. Even if you are not a reading champ yourself, you can be curious about what your child is reading and talk about it. You both should expect that things make sense. When things do not make sense, you can reinforce audiobook strategies by pausing and using technology to look things up. Your mantra? "Let's find out." Remember, no guessing without confirming!

Whatever reading technology you are using, from tablet readers to print books, it is important to keep track of a child's thinking as they go. By later elementary school, they will be expected to show evidence for their thinking about what they read. You can use digital highlighting, sticky notes, and the commenting feature in Google Docs to do this. A five-slide presentation (Title/Beginning/Middle/End/Bibliography) can capture stories and give children a chance to illustrate their thinking. This way they can make a library of reviews for books they have read. Your child's teachers or the tech team at school will have lots of other app suggestions if your child doesn't offer them first. Encourage your child to look up words using a thesaurus extension or app. That way they start with something they already know. It is a great way to build more extensive vocabulary.

Writing Skills: The Challenge of Putting it Altogether

Writing is often taught as a process or set of steps, as shown in Table 5:

Table 5: Writing Steps

STEP	HOW TO DO IT
Prewrite	Determine the purpose. Decide who it is for. Generate ideas. Sort and label categories of ideas. Choose a pattern such as compare/contrast, explaining a process, or giving examples. Make a basic organizational plan using a step-wise graphic organizer to collect ideas.
Write	Use your plan to compose sentences. Fluently retrieve vocabulary to get your ideas across. Create paragraphs that stick to one idea. Support a point of view with evidence. Use reasonable spelling, standard grammar, and mechanics.
Revise	Consider the piece from the point of view of the intended reader. Ask a peer for input at this stage. Make changes in organization and word choice. Add details. Read aloud to hear the language. Use the "Comments" function in your word processor to keep track of your thinking. Use an electronic thesaurus for word variety.
Edit	Identify and correctly fix mechanical errors so that every sentence can stand alone. Read whole sentences from the end to the beginning in order to focus on one sentence at a time. Use the spelling and grammar checker, but know that it is not perfect. Ask an expert, not a peer, to help with mechanics at this stage. Consult the rubric if you have been given one.
Publish	Submit the final copy for whatever publication purpose you need. Evaluate your writing experience. Did you stay on track throughout the writing process?

There are several ways to explore why your child struggles with writing as well as numerous ways to help. Some students struggle with language skills, not just the writing process, and need significant structure to plan and organize their thinking.

Others have general ideas but struggle to add details or support their thoughts with evidence. Does your child avoid writing, perhaps by waiting until the last minute to begin or by claiming they did not know or forgot about an assignment? If this happens on a rare occasion, you might overlook it. Disregard whether they are telling the truth and ask them questions that start with "What." Here is a possible parent-child dialogue. Each pair below begins with the parent coaching question:

"What writing assignments do you have this week?"
"Let's see... English Essay, Science Lab, History."

"What assignment will you start with?"
"The English is one page. Easy. I'll do it first."

"What are the directions to follow?"
"Tell about a person I admire and why."

"What is the first step you can take?"
"I don't know. Think of a person?"

"What does the rubric look like?"
"The teacher didn't give us one."

"What resources do you need to get started?"
"I guess I should read the directions."

"What can I do to support you?"
"Who do you think I admire?"

"What will it be like when you are done?"
"A relief, since there are two more things to do!"

Table 6 lists writing challenges on the left and strategies that parents might suggest on the right.

Table 6: Strategies to Meet Writing Challenges

WRITING CHALLENGE	STRATEGY
Getting started/Deciding what to write about	Offer two or three choices that fit the assignment.
Going off-topic while writing	Suggest writing the main idea at the top of the page and highlighting it.
Running out of ideas for a topic	Suggest generating a list of ideas in advance rather than while writing.
Writing about random rather than connected ideas	Suggest organizing the list of ideas into categories before writing and/or color-coding different categories of ideas.
Starting sentences in similar ways	Give transition words (First, Then, Next, After that, Finally...) or "how" adverbs (Suddenly, Usually, Unexpectedly, Quickly, Carefully, Secretly...) to use as sentence starters.
Not answering the prompt or missing some implied directions	Suggest breaking down assignment into sequential steps and numbering them.
Having many mechanical errors	Suggest: Double-spacing all writing. Errors are easier to spot that way. Using detective skills while proofreading. Putting a dot in the left margin for each error in a line. Four errors? Put four dots. None?

Math Patterns

Math is full of patterns. The image in Figure 4 might look to you like a grid, a quilt, or a window lying flat. Maybe it is a garden plot or a retaining wall.

Figure 4: Math Grid

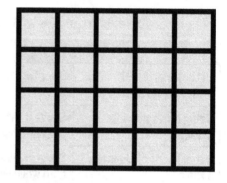

In math it is called a rectangular array. You can describe it using words or numbers. Four by five. 4 x 5. You can count the boxes. There are 20. Thus, a four by five array has twenty boxes in it. The math fact 4 x 5 = 20 and the multiplication table result when you slide your fingers from the outside until they meet at 20 are all the same thing.

If you count by 5's on your fingers, the fourth finger will be 20. If you have four nickels worth 5 cents each you will have 20 cents. On an analog clock you can tell time by 5 minutes, up to 55 minutes each hour. Each multiple of five will fall on the number of its fact family friend: 20 minutes past the hour will fall on the 4, and 35 minutes past the hour will fall on 7.

Children need to learn patterns like these for math as well as ones for reading. To master the times tables, they are often encouraged to practice until the answers become automatic. This can be effortful, and some children will find their memory storage and retrieval inaccurate. Introducing students to the pattern of a rectangular array can make the multiplication table more than a reference sheet. This can reinforce meaningful retrieval and make the multiplication table more than merely a look-up tool. Most children will benefit from having math concepts directly connected to their visual-spatial world so they can construct practical uses for them rather than merely memorizing them.

Developing Reasoning Skills: Accommodations versus Strategies

How can you know whether underdeveloped skills may be contributing to lack of motivation and lower-than-expected performance? Sometimes, as in the case of Kai, general education accommodations have been put in place that make it possible for your child to move through the curriculum and get their schoolwork done. These adjustments do not teach missing skills, though, and they can even mask real problems until a student is in a new learning context, like a different grade, school, or even college.

Accommodations are like booster seats at the learning table. A common example is extended time. Another would be audio books or speech-to-text. Accommodations by-pass underdeveloped reading decoding, fluency, and comprehension skills so that the student does not miss out on the content and concepts of learning in the curriculum. The goal is to prevent a lack of skills from inhibiting learning of foundational content.

Some accommodations involve providing important cues in the learning environment, such as having a word wall filled with commonly misspelled words or a math reference sheet with commonly used formulas. Other accommodations adjust time or presentation of learning materials.

While accommodations can be helpful, some accommodations can make a student appear more skillful than they actually

are. Table 7 shows three basic kinds of classroom accommodations with a few examples. Accommodations can be customized to meet the needs of any learner.

Table 7: Common Accommodations

Target	Examples
Environment	Seat: Near place of primary instruction; with appropriate peers; away from distractions
	Classroom: Designed with consistency and routine in mind
	Resources: Color-coded and clearly labeled resources in classroom
	Offer movement breaks
Instruction/Presentation	Preview new concepts and connect explicitly to previous material
	Provide visual and verbal information simultaneously
	Break down complex directions
	Provide access to audiobooks and other multimedia
Assignments/ Assessment	Allow use of a calculator or reference sheet
	Give extended time and teach how to use it
	Speech-to-text/dictation allowed for written work
	Provide graphic organizers across all subjects
	Connect examples of completed work to rubrics

How to Use Accommodations at Home

You can try similar accommodations at home. Parents are
often very good at accommodations for non-academic purposes. Think of the many ways that you cue your child to
do things needed to get through the day as part of a family.

Certain things are put in consistent places or happen in a certain order. Sometimes you are providing needed structure for health and safety. Other times you just need to get to places on time or facilitate play dates.

Accommodations can be even more helpful if you keep track of the ones that you are using and monitor their effectiveness. Aim for fading support, which means offering the accommodation less and less when underlying skills do become more fully developed.

CONCLUSION

Remember that sometimes you are accommodating a skill challenge so that content is not missed. Other times you are teaching to be sure that the skill is being developed.

Accommodations should not take the place of learning skills. It is always important both to acquire content and learn skills. Not feeling confident about doing this yourself? Your child may need more explicit teaching and how-to strategies, not just a reminder, by-pass, or cueing system.

Sometimes teachers are very open to trying different things to move children along in their skill acquisition. Other times they are pretty sure that if they wait it out, a student will be ready later on.

There is no reason to wait. Meet your child where they are right now. Keep feeding your child's learning needs with skills and strategies that keep them both motivated and able to learn more with increasing independence.

INKLING 6

Who is Responsible When Students Do Not Learn?

When I got my first real job after graduate school, it was at a boarding school for students with dyslexia. This school was for children who had stayed below the radar before their lack of skills doomed them to school failure. Imagine a school that you had to fail to get into! The director at this school up-ended everything I had been told about education during my student teaching. She made it abundantly clear who was responsible for student learning: I was.

In every training session that happened for months at lunchtime in her office, she boomed, "If the student has not learned, the teacher has not taught." This was a heavy responsibility, one that I was not sure I wanted, but I soaked up every trick and strategy that could help turn children into winners at the game of learning.

In that school, carefully trained teachers created individualized, structured, yet flexible lessons. All school activities built confidence and community. There was horseback riding, studio art, woodshop, and public speaking, as well as a variety of individual and team sports. Importantly, there was no expectation of perfection, only of improvement guided through deliberate practice, careful measurement, and frequent incremental feedback. The results were gains of several years' worth of academic skills in only months of schooling. It was not a miracle. It was a system. This meant it could be replicated.

The children amazed me by how smart they were, considering that some of the incoming high schoolers barely had third-grade academic skills. Some students still stand out to me. One student wanted to be a science fiction writer. He was a struggling reader and writer, but in his head were endless stories that he at first dictated to me and later wrote himself. His spoken vocabulary was astounding. His background knowledge was exceptional. The spelling and sentence structure were original. Fortunately, there were strategies for that.

In the art studio, students created paintings and sculptures that revealed their visual spatial imagination and talents. In the woodshop they designed perfectly balanced chairs and, in one case, a gorgeous sailboat that the artist went on to build and launch. Science experiments involved hands-on work and utilized sketching skills. There were both written reports and creative visual representations of results. Everyone learned to present findings to an audience and take feedback.

While not everyone was a fantastic athlete, everyone played on a team and improved skills. Students could develop individual lifetime sports like tennis, running, skiing, swimming, and golf.

The average length of stay was three school years. No matter their age on arrival, the students tended to go off successfully, albeit with tutorial support, to mainstream schools and higher education.

CHAPTER 7
....

Learn How to Game the Systems of School

Practically every child can play video games. To do so, they've learned skills, strategies, adaptability, and persistence. This chapter is about reorienting some of those key abilities when the game of school requires skills that make it difficult for students to achieve competence. It specifically addresses what students must be able to do with technology and why this is often overwhelming, even for digital natives. Some solutions cause new problems. You will learn when to wait and when to ask for more help.

The School Game

Each school year can be like competing in a multiplayer video game that levels up when a student may not have. The game begins with a sense of adventure and opportunities for discovery. Children are introduced to new allies, the instructors and teammates who will teach them skills and knowledge for developing character and instincts. There may be enemies of time or difficulty or misunderstanding while students work together and separately to level up.

To succeed at the game of school requires the efficient development of early skills for reading, handwriting, written language, math facts, and math reasoning as well as patterns for social expectation, self-regulation, and work production. If a child struggles at the early elementary level, there is often support, at least for a while. If each grade level represents student success as measured by the game metrics of grades and passing, we tend to believe that a student is learning. This makes the end of each school year feel like a win.

However, each time a child moves up a level, important bits of their student story stay behind. Teachers and parents are often just as relieved as students to have a school year over. Adults may mistakenly believe students will outgrow challenges the way they outgrow clothing, learn to try harder, and eventually find their sweet spot in school. Maybe the right teacher will connect with them, and a passion will be born. Or at least they will have completed a requirement, gained some transcript health, and maybe never need to take that subject again. In this way school is like a game, with some parts of the realm wide open while other paths lead to *Game Over.*

Pressing Pause: I Encounter Video Games

When my son was in middle school, he thought I should learn to play video games. Before this I had never used a video game controller. There was so much to learn! I felt breathless from being chased. I could not see the being that was threatening me, but I could hear it breathing and feel the vibration of its every footfall in surround sound. Suddenly it was running faster, and I did not know if I could escape. I did not know the being's skills, powers, health, or advantages, or if its range included the entire world or just a focused area. Because I was in an open world, the path ahead was up to me. But every choice had an unknown consequence.

I needed the entire game to slow down to less than half speed while I simultaneously used buttons and a joystick to keep my avatar from missing the finish line forever. Because I had no skills for the game, my performance was deeply embarrassing, and while I was willing to watch my son play, I cringed at the thought of playing more. Undeterred, over several years he patiently chose different games that had puzzles or learning as part of the success pathway. I was now in charge of how quickly or slowly I moved in a world, but I found identifying the numerous hidden rules and patterns frustrating. Eventually he tried to convert me to game development as an art form. I could move at my leisure, wandering virtual worlds where I did not have to play too much.

Could I have developed the needed skills? Without them I could not succeed. Could I have managed additional hostile antagonists? That would have been important because believing I had the power to overcome them might have been the key to saving my virtual life. Could I have designed needed tools and weapons? Foraged for food while staying safe from attack? Fortunately, my game controller had a pause button, and calamity could be averted, at least temporarily. In real life, however, there often is no pause button. The only way to avoid looming destruction may be to escape what feels threatening.

While I did not become a successful Twitch streamer, I did realize some important and humbling lessons from my attempt to play video games. I lacked basic motor skills for playing. It was like being unable to use a pen when I needed to write an entire document in perfect calligraphy. Despite having a multifunctional game controller and a patient teacher, I was a minimally functional player.

Once I had decided that learning gaming skills was not for me, it was very difficult to improve. I still remember the three choices I made about learning to game.

1. **I would play but not practice** since I was not really getting better.

2. **I would give up caring** since my avatar never made it to the finish line.

3. **I would stop trying to learn** since my avatar seemed destined for disintegration.

My frustration was about more than needing to learn basic skills. I also did not intuitively figure out the rules and patterns for surviving in a virtual room. While I believed that given all the time in the world, I might be able to learn those skills, raw optimism was not enough. I was so behind in my learning curve that I could not maintain the drive to get better at playing. I felt like no amount of effort could protect my avatar who was stuck in a virtual world full of resources I could not access, destined to be eliminated by powers greater than my own.

Digital Natives: Consumers and Producers

Even before COVID-19, much of the school curriculum had moved to digital platforms. While this is a triumph of technology, it also means content and tools are hidden under layers of classroom management software. Yes, this expands access to a world of online resources and even keeps fields like ancient history regularly updated with new ways to think about the accomplishments and imperfections of our ancestors. Content mounted in an online repository can be searched by a machine, copied and pasted with a few clicks, and potentially cross-checked with information on millions of other pages.

Adults often expect that children will intuitively pick up how to locate and complete work online because they have been exposed to so much technology. You may even think that your digitally native child would be a natural success with online learning approaches. Why, then, does learning become so difficult for some children once they are past the more hands-on early elementary years of school?

Outside of school, children are mostly consumers of technology. They have devices of all sorts. They watch streaming shows, YouTube, and TikTok videos. They message and video chat with their friends using the latest apps and filters. They boss Alexa and Siri around the Internet of Things. They play video games, customize their devices, and learn hacking skills to access websites their parents do not want them to see. Their ability to use technology creatively makes it easy to argue that when it comes to schoolwork troubles, they are just not trying hard enough. But riffing with your phone apps or crushing it at Minecraft, or whatever else is hot, is not the same as schoolwork.

While a student's job at school does involve consuming learning, they must also become producers. The days are gone when students had assignments handed directly to them by their teachers and put in backpacks to remove at home ready to complete, all with embedded structure such as directions on a worksheet. Now a student must manage what I call the *Producer's Checklist* to get work done.

Table 8: Items in the Producer's Checklist

☐ Remember login and password.

☐ Log into portal.

☐ Check the assignments dashboard to see what's new.

☐ Make notes (in some way – mental?) of tasks.

☐ Go to individual course tabs to find assignments, resources, and links.

☐ Discover what is due soonest and potentially record that in a planner (digital or paper).

☐ Use a variety of apps and websites to complete a single assignment.

☐ Research and be able to tell what is salient without a teacher or textbook telling them.

☐ Self-teach with video.

☐ Make a personalized file management system.

☐ Set up new files and save them to the right folders.

☐ Make a work plan for the day, week, and future.

☐ Stay on track while doing individual assignments.

☐ Use self-regulation and self-help behaviors.

☐ Complete work online, including responding in a group chat.

☐ Contact group members without becoming distracted by non-work chatter.

☐ Submit work when it is completed.

☐ Check separate portal for graded work if a teacher uses such system.

☐ Keep a running learner's log of material since just doing assignments is not enough.

☐ Know what information to retain.

☐ Become increasingly aware of how their own learning process works.

Online systems require a variety of embedded skills that are assumed but not explicitly taught. This is the short list. Every day I see students who must do all of these things plus a variety of steps within their actual assignments to remember, retrieve, apply, and reimagine learning. Perhaps you can imagine how having a learning, attention, or executive function challenge can make digital systems for finding and managing schoolwork feel overwhelming, before the real work even begins. Part of the difficulty is that there isn't usually a standard way of delivering assignments that all teachers follow, since different subject matter and teaching styles lend themselves to different uses of technology.

Just imagine how this short list can be compounded by processing or working memory struggles. Elementary schoolers can often produce solid work in lower grades because there is, quite simply, less work and more structure. But older students who depend on this structure may be at a disadvantage when more independence and skills application are expected. At home parents may find it challenging to help children plan ahead, preview topics, or make connections between school and real-world learning.

Overcoming a Personal Resistance: Hunter's Story

During the COVID-19 quarantine I met a new client who was a high school senior. My objective for the first session with Hunter was to extract some potentially painful information from the student gently, without any direct confrontation.

"So how is quarantine working out for you?"
"Oh, there's nothing to do. My sleep schedule is off, and school keeps sending work. Like I'm going to do any of that."

"Is not doing the work a choice?"

"I'm making it one."

"Sure. I understand. Do you have your work in a portal? Some people I meet with have one of those."

"Yeah. But I never go in there. The system sends email to my parents if something is actually important. They yell at me and...yeah."

"Can you show me what your portal is like?"

"If you want to see it. But I don't even know the password."

Fast forward to session three, and Hunter had recovered the password, shown me the dashboard of missing work, and was startled to discover that there were 54 missing assignments listed in the portal. Even in my world, where one of the reasons I see students is that they are not doing their work, this was a lot of work to complete, especially since more work was still being assigned every day. There were only six weeks left of school. Could the semester be saved?

I knew what *not* to ask:

- "How could you get so far behind?"

- "Why don't you just do the work and get it over with?"

- "Why can't you just do the work like everyone else?"

- "Don't you realize that you could fail and never get into a good college?"

Instead, I listened for Hunter's background noise, the stories that they were telling to get permission not to act. People will go to great lengths to win, especially when their rights have been violated. Anger, the unfairness emotion, has a tendency to make people want to hold back, push back, or even fight. Hunter's unfairness script sounded like this:

- *I should not have to do work that I hate.*

- *It's all just busywork because no one knows what to do with us.*

- *It says this is optional. Only stupid people waste their time with optional work.*

- *This work is a waste of my time since I will never need any of it.*

- *I wanted to be in art, not computer science. If I was in art, I wouldn't have this homework.*

- *Kids mostly don't get sick with COVID. Nobody I know is sick. It's stupid to close school.*

- *I shouldn't have to do work when there are no grades since grades are all that matters.*

- *It says that this work won't change the grade from earlier in the term, so why do it?*

These thoughts, powered by anger, were the permission Hunter needed to avoid work. What Hunter was missing as they made this choice was the ability to see the future cost of not completing work.

It is very easy to project your fears onto your child who has already stopped trying. Hunter's parents may have felt powerless to help as the cliff of graduation approached. To them, the work needed for success was within view, but the deep cost of their child's potential failure was ever present.

You might think that a line of questioning which asks your child to think about a bleak future is a practical, logical approach that will motivate a child to take action. Instead, it floods them with your fear, given they just cannot answer your questions. Now they are terrified as well as angry, and they may not trust your motives in offering help. These fear-filled thoughts are not the emotional recipe for getting work started. Questions like, "What if you don't graduate?" and "How will you get into a good college?" just get the answer, "I don't know."

Trying requires at least some future-mindedness. Faced with utter failure and the impossibility of pleasing their parents, Hunter could not see a path forward.

But that was not the end of the story. Remember all that missing work? Within five weeks, the 54 assignments and all of the other incoming ones were completed. This happened before the actual deadline, so Hunter received credit for the semester and graduated on time. It happened without threats, rules, or shaming because those approaches would only have fueled the emotion storms of anger, fear, and embarrassment. Hunter needed what any student does when faced with over-whelming amounts of work: curiosity, hope, and pride, as well as some supportive planning.

Supportive Planning

Here's what supportive planning can sound like, illustrated with snippets of my conversations with Hunter about getting the work done.

Me: "If I set the timer for five minutes, what could be finished when it goes off?"

Hunter: "Spanish vocab."

Me: "Let's go to that assignment. I'm starting the timer now."

Me: "What is the smallest assignment that you can finish?"

Hunter: "Math."

Me: "How much can you finish in five minutes? I can set a timer if you like."

Me: "What assignment would make you feel proud if you were done with it?"

Hunter: "CompSci."

Me: "What is your time estimate for that?"

Hunter: "An hour. I have to code to make this car move in S-curves."

Me: "Should we break it up into 10-minute sections?"

Hunter: "OK."

Me: "What assignment would make you feel relieved if you finished it?"

Hunter: "The English paper."

Me: "I'm sorry that one is stressful. Do you have a graphic organizer? We can use yours or I can set one up while you are finishing the math."

At the end of this lesson, Hunter had learned how long assignments might take to complete, as little as five minutes or as long as several hours when planned in advance. Using dialogue like this, students can discover that long things feel shorter when broken up into shorter, stepwise parts. They can learn that doing what they like feels better when they are not also carrying around the weight of avoidance. Students are often willing to work with a non-judgmental adult.

In Hunter's case, this still did not motivate learning since the goal was merely to complete missing assignments and avoid impending disaster. Learning what Hunter could do independently, not just producing work that was required by others, was still a missing ingredient.

Barriers to Helping

When it seems to you like your child may just need a study boost, how do you help? Let's consider math. The early elementary school teacher may have emailed home a weekly newsletter about the topics the class is learning, for example two-digit subtraction with regrouping, multiplication facts up to twelve, using arrays to solve real-world problems. This kind of specific teacher-generated communication to parents tends to decrease with grade level because student independence is expected to increase.

For your middle school or older student, you will have parent access to the school's online portal, but since you are not in class with your child every day, you are probably missing some key information for managing teacher expectations. As a result, it may be hard to help your child study for a test because you can't consult the book for the sequence of math skills that were taught or find related pages in a workbook.

Sometimes teachers have a scope and sequence assigned to them that makes it very clear what they need to be teaching. This is the *what* and *when* of learning. It is a cookbook of sorts, but it is not a textbook. In earlier times, teachers made hard copy lesson plans. Those resources now live in the virtual world. This seems like an efficient way to store and deliver a variety of student work, and it appears to reduce dependence on printed textbooks, which can quickly become outdated. To take advantage of this, parents need to be able to guide a child to find resources and assignments efficiently. "Where was that tab?" "How does this online book work?" "What page was that assignment on?" "This is due tomorrow?"

This can test both students and their parents. If your children have already reached a stage characterized by questioning if their parents get it, they may resist help. The processes that you learned in math may also be very different from the ones your child is now expected to use.

Some Solutions Cause New Problems: Nikhil's Story

One of the most mystifying things that parents of a struggling student hear in a school meeting is that their child is "able to work at grade level" and is "in the average range." With a little more effort, things can turn around, right? How can that be, you wonder, if your child struggles to be consistent? Forgets the spelling words right after the test? Doesn't seem to understand the directions? Forgets what was supposedly learned during the school day? Can't get their multiplication facts to stick no matter how many flashcard apps you try?

When Nikhil was in fourth grade, he opened the door of the moving car his mother was driving and threw himself out onto the road. While this was not the first impulsive thing he had ever done, it was definitely the scariest. Fortunately, like some character in a video game, he landed on soft grass and rolled, unhurt. Thereafter Nikhil's parents made sure that their car's child safety locks were always on.

Nikhil was also impulsive at school. Teachers noted that he was quite bright but did not try hard enough. The school psychologist tested him and told Nikhil's parents that he had adequate skills and ability, so there was no apparent learning-based reason for failing to do his schoolwork. This information was delivered as good news with the implication that Nikhil could turn it around. By the time Nikhil was in 6th grade, though, the school was recommending that he go to summer school because he was so far behind with assignments. Failure to do his work had become a discipline problem. Nikhil was regularly sent to the internal suspension room with his incomplete work. More effort and clear consequences were the offered solutions, yet Nikhil completed few assignments. At the rate Nikhil was slipping, the school warned, the twelve-year-old would never graduate from high school.

In Nikhil's imagination, he had already dropped out of high school. Learning wasn't for him. His parents believed that the school's evaluations of their son's skills meant the diagnosis, "bright and lazy." They gave him productivity apps, tutoring both privately and at school, and planners to keep track of the work that he was not doing. After sixth grade, he refused to return to school and instead was homeschooled to avoid repeating the year.

To increase Nikhil's learning, his mother, who was not a trained teacher, diligently read to him. They practiced flashcards and solved real-life math problems together: cooking, household budgeting, repair bills. He gained solid background knowledge from enriching family conversations and with family friends from multiple cultures. He learned the check-in process with the home health aide when his father was ill. But Nikhil still had third-grade-level independent literacy and math skills. He could not type more than a few inaccurately spelled words per minute, and his only solid computer skills were for playing video games. As he competed successfully against players all over the globe, Nikhil imagined himself navigating many virtual worlds.

Unfortunately, some solutions may cause new problems. Online gaming offered Nikhil some much-needed self-esteem, but it came at the cost of regular sleep, healthy eating habits, and related self-regulation. Nikhil needed a future story of successful learning coupled with hope that he could one day be a successful adult. When Nikhil was referred to me, he was fifteen years old. He would be a legal adult in just three years. Could he learn nine years of skills or more in that amount of time? What could his future look like?

Nikhil did not get help he needed in high school, so we decided the best step would be to drop out. He did not have the skills to do the work, pass classes, or graduate.

After dropping out at age sixteen, Nikhil had time and energy to make up skills. I continued to coach him and help him learn missing content. He learned numerous missing skills and caught up with peers so that he passed all high school equivalency subject tests for his state on the first try before turning eighteen. Then he worked for two years in retail and construction. He enlisted in the military before his twentieth birthday and scored so high on the military aptitude test that he was able to choose his career path: US Army Intelligence. He also learned how to exit (relatively safely) a moving (flying!) vehicle (at night!) in Army Jump School and has begun college courses to support his career in military intelligence. He also teaches new recruits.

CONCLUSION

Online aspects of school can be overwhelming before students even get started with their actual assignments. By providing supportive planning and asking non-judgmental questions, you can help them imagine winning the game of school. Like Nikhil, your child needs for you to have a hopeful future story for them. It is never too early; start now.

INKLING 7

Inspired By Their Own Potential

The school for students with dyslexia that I described in Inkling 6 opened my eyes to successful ways to educate children with learning disabilities. I wondered, were there children like them when I was in elementary or middle school? Did they start out loving school and then get siphoned off into a different hallway? Did they learn to hate school? Why and when did the trouble start for them? What happened to other children who did not get help?

Whatever they may have lacked, my students in that special school and others like them learned to be inspired by their own potential rather than embarrassed by their bewildering failures. With the right strategic teaching approaches, these children were successful.

I learned from my students, and I always asked questions. What worked for them? What strengths had they used? What had failed them? How could I change small things for bigger learning, engagement, and impact? I also asked myself questions about what I observed. Were there things that worked for everyone, or was all learning individual?

During the first twenty years of my professional life, even when I was a school-based teacher and later a program founder or director, I always had a private practice where I saw parents and students. I learned many new skills to apply by independently studying dyslexia education, learning theories, neurodevelopment, and psychology. My professional life gave me access to colleagues in the growing field of learning differences. I explored the connections between self-efficacy, social-emotional learning, and achievement. I also married and had children. I never underestimate the impact that having children has had on my views about learning and human nature!

CHAPTER 8

Manage Executive Functions and Procrastination

It is important to understand the thinking, organization, and self-control skills that people apply to solve challenging problems. These are called *executive functions (EFs)*. If your child's executive functions lag behind, your resilience and coaching parent skills are essential here because your child needs support rather than judgment. There are ways to help children learn more efficient and effective use of their executive functions. This learning often moves them away from procrastination. You can also help your child connect already successful extra-curricular use of executive function to their academic endeavors.

Solving Complex Problems Takes More than Academic Skills

When we are faced with challenging problems requiring complex, multi-step solutions, we rely on *executive function* (EF) skills. These brain-based abilities involve both awareness of what's needed and the ability to take intentional action. Examples include planning ahead with the end in mind, stopping one task, starting another, and staying focused while working. A list of the EFs commonly used in school appears in Table 9 on page page 149.

By using executive functions to address a complex question, a child can make a preliminary plan to gather information, even when they are completely inexperienced with the task. If a child has difficulties with any of the executive function skills, they may struggle at many points, from stopping what they are doing now, to switching to the next task, to actually starting the work of planning and then staying focused on the steps of a task.

What are the Executive Functions?

Table 9 is a chart of the eight kinds of executive functions organized as a sequence of steps required to complete a task successfully. Your child may struggle with some and be quite competent with others. You may be so good at all of them that you are blissfully unaware of how much brain power goes into managing all the tasks you need to complete. No wonder you can be so exhausted at the end of a day!

Your child, at any age, is still developing executive functions. Whether you remember it or not, you developed your executive functions over time and with practice, too.

The first three steps, Stop-Switch-Start, not only happen in order but happen over and over while the other steps are also happening. As you read through the chart, imagine how challenging it could be for children who get stuck in between stopping, switching, and starting, particularly if they struggle with any of the other behaviors needed along the way. Not only would this be exhausting, they might have little interest in doing it again and again for a whole school year, especially with increasingly complex tasks and unfamiliar content.

Table 9: The Executive Functions Explained

Keyword and Purpose	What you do when it is going well
STOP present behavior • Create physical and emotional space for doing something else • Control impulses to continue the previous activity	• Make attention available • Put aside worrying, playing, socializing, eating, other work, or resisting
SWITCH to new activity • Select next step, resource, skill, or activity • Can be very effortful when it is not happening smoothly • Harder with unfamiliar skills, resources, activities, or tasks • Staying on one task can involve a lot of switches	• Switch attention smoothly from step to step, resource to resource, and task to task • Do it in the background with little effort • Do it without conscious management • Resist getting stuck • Note: Math, reading comprehension, and written language rely heavily on switching skills
START an activity • Figure out at least one clear action step that you do not resist • Begin work	• Work backwards from outcome to figure out what comes first • For single-step tasks: Just get started • For multi-step tasks: Manage anxiety, anger, sadness that can lead to procrastination

Keyword and Purpose	What you do when it is going well
REGULATE thoughts and emotions • Develop awareness of emotions • Stay focused • Check for background noise • Understand and manage own resistance	• Keep energy high to get work done • Use effective strategies • Employ resilient thinking • Maintain long-term perspective and goal orientation
GENERATE ideas and establish steps • Know what's needed to move forward, including time • Do What, How, When • Uncover embedded directions	• Envision desired outcomes • Convert assignments into a form that can guide steps • Estimate time • Apply lessons learned from previous successes
HOLD right information in mind • Manage distractions • Store new information temporarily • Remember long enough to use it now, before forgetting	• Use memory space and strategies optimally • Manage own personal memory capacity, whether it is vast like a Thanksgiving platter or tiny like a tapas plate
ORGANIZE resources • Have what is needed, when and where needed • Store like things together with later retrieval in mind	• Use checklists, spreadsheets, bins, shelves, online resources, reminders, notifications • Use system for remembering what's in notebooks, computer files, desk, locker, work area, bedroom
CONNECT behavior to effective outcomes • Apply work, social, time behaviors • Collect performance data	• Learn from feedback • Make adjustments • Check work against: List/Directions, Rubric, Exemplar • Self-advocate

Using Questions to Guide Executive Functions

In school, children are expected to engage in *inquiry*. That's the part of the curriculum that encourages curiosity, questioning, and follow-up research. For younger students, teachers often provide reading materials that children use to answer guiding questions. As students move up through the grades, they are expected to be able to generate their own lines of questioning, organize the information they encounter, and present their findings, all with decreasing support. Activities that children have probably never considered before are useful for helping to explore and develop executive function skills. It is important for students to reflect on their learning and record it in some way for further reflection.

Executive Functions in Motion: Moving a Giraffe

Having a solid but flexible plan with goals, structure, intermediate objectives, and resilient thinking is key before you try to accomplish something big, especially for the first time. When I was a classroom teacher, I called this way of thinking *moving a giraffe*. Where would you begin if you really did need to move one? The answer depends on developmental age, experience, and executive functioning. When I ask students this question, a first grader is likely to rely on imagination. Their solutions might be impractical and even funny to adults, since children this age cannot conceptualize the whole host of possible steps to consider. "I'd use a leash," they might answer in all seriousness.

Somewhat older elementary school students are used to having adults provide structure and scaffolding, so they often do not get too far from real answers. They might start by saying, "I don't know." They are still fairly concrete in their problem solving at this age and may rely heavily on their own experience (or lack of it) to help with solutions and planning. They usually imagine that there is probably at least one right answer. Not knowing it right away, they may not even venture a guess. Some intrepid problem solvers may begin searching for it. Others might not be willing to risk a guess without directions for where to look.

By early middle school, a curious child usually knows to wonder, *How could I find out?* Some of them will type the question about moving a giraffe into their Internet browser without prompting to see if there is anything on the first-page results that might prove a short-cut to the answer. They might impulsively respond to one of the first answers they see.

By high school, a student will typically work backwards, consulting the assignment rubric to see why they are being asked this in the first place. They will know to ask who else has already moved a giraffe and will choose to learn from what others have posted, especially on YouTube, where they can be entertained while seeing the job being done in the shortest time possible.

Table 10 shows a simple graphic organizer with the topics some sixth graders generated for the following assignment I gave them: "How do you move a giraffe? Has this been done before? Where can you find out? Record what you learn."

As you can see, there was a lot of information to collect and then organize, even with groups of children tackling topics a few at a time and sharing with the rest of the group. Collecting information was just a start.

Table 10: Student Graphic Organizer for How to Move a Giraffe

Find out about giraffes	Where Information Found: Paraphrase
Size/Height	
Gender	
Age	
Food	
Life span	
Locations To/From	
Distance	
Purpose	
Rules/Permission	
Cost	
Materials	
Tools needed	
Transportation	
People needed	

When doing assignments like this, some students will be excited to proceed and happily read, research, and record. While they do this intentional information gathering, they may also be learning incidentally. The giraffe movers can pick up bits of interesting information and build skills that are not explicitly requested. If you were observing the class, you'd think those working students were the ones on task. Other students might seem confused, distracted, or disengaged.

To move a giraffe, it will not be enough just to collect information. The steps will need to be shaped into a sequential plan that takes into account what must happen as well as what may happen at each point along the way. At some point, the experiences of other successful giraffe movers may also become helpful.

Executive function growth is important both for getting work done and learning how to learn content. All students are works in progress, and they develop executive functions at different rates.

When Executive Functions Go Missing

Perhaps your child struggles with transitions. They may find it hard to stop one activity, switch attention, and start another task. Perhaps they do not yet know how to generate ideas and steps to determine the help they need and how to ask for it. Some behaviors, such as self-advocacy, are not always easy for students. Perhaps they are embarrassed. They may struggle to connect asking for help to effective outcomes. Maybe their basic skills are not quite up to the task of independent inquiry. In a group activity, a task like moving a giraffe can make it possible for children with different levels of EF development to work together. Children can rely on others to do the parts that are most difficult for them, but still be able to contribute by doing tasks that come more easily to them, such as finding pictures for a future slideshow.

During the stay-at-home phases of the COVID-19 pandemic, remote and hybrid learning gave new meaning to self-help. This kind of curriculum presentation is not going away. It can be challenging in terms of executive function because so many resources need to be collected just to get started. The need for executive functions is not only embedded in directions for assignments. It is also buried in what is sometimes called the *hidden curriculum* because it is hidden in online documents, often with directions and rubrics written as curriculum standards in teacher-language. With these challenges, children may struggle to find, complete, and turn in work independently. It is also increasingly challenging for many parents to know how to help at home.

Even in the same school or same course, different teachers use technology in so many different ways that students may miss out on content that they could learn, sometimes missing entire assignments. Even a student with well-developed executive functions can find schoolwork mentally and emotionally exhausting because every shift in direction and switch in thinking consumes working memory capacity.

Every switch can lead to a cycle of forgetting, resulting in frustration and self-doubt. For example, every time a student leaves a webpage and navigates to a new one, what was on the previous page may be pushed out of working memory. This increases the number of times a page or concept must be revisited. This by itself can make it laborious to process and remember information. Any student, even one with solid skills, can slip off-task. Stop. Switch. Start. It needs to happen over and over, with every thought and page click. The student making A's in elementary school where assignments were smaller, structure was higher, and expectations were more relaxed, may become anxious, disorganized, and disengaged.

Executive function challenges can look like distraction, discipline problems, disorganization, or carelessness. It is important to withhold judgment and begin by being generous, acting as if a student just needs some structure and cueing. Unless you have specific diagnoses, you may not know if specific learning, emotional, and attention factors are complicating the picture. The student who struggles needs support, not judgment, when they make mistakes, especially if there are multiple tasks required for doing the work.

Managing Emotions

Never underestimate the impact that being cold, hungry, or tired can have on someone's ability to stick to even the best-designed plan. Sometimes the plan will just not work, no matter how well-thought out it may be. Being grouchy and uncooperative? That can happen. You may think that you and teachers have set your child up for success with daily calendars, checklists, and graphic organizers. All your child has to do is follow directions. Except that being overwhelmed by emotion is like facing the snowstorms of life. Maybe a task will seem small to you, but to your child it could seem like clearing snow from a parking lot with only a shovel.

A major aspect of executive function involves the ability to continue being productive while feeling and managing emotions of all kinds. Your child may experience long, boring days at school when they feel they are presented with content that seems unconnected to real life. At school there is often low choice, low opportunity for creativity, and low freedom to do assignments in different ways. At the same time, school is perceived to be a very high stakes endeavor where performance is pivotal to a foggy future. Students regularly end their school day feeling stressed. Many parents observe that homework time is characterized by irritability, inattention, inconsistency, low motivation, and task avoidance. All students, not just ones with learning, attention, and executive function challenges, can experience cognitive fatigue from managing the many competing demands for their focus.

Working Memory: When Size Matters

Are you open to the possibility that what looks like pushback from your child may instead be cognitive and emotional overload? Consider working memory, for example. I think of memory in terms of plate sizes, which range from tiny plates to enormous platters. For a child with a small plate size for information, studying is like going to an American Thanksgiving meal with only a tapas plate. Only a few tiny bits can be held on it. Perhaps they try to juggle separate plates. With so many needs to Stop-Switch-Start, the meal will be frustrating.

The student with less working memory capacity may work with speed and impulsivity. It's a way to try to make up for the vague awareness that they will quickly forget. This approach can appear to sacrifice accuracy, but students probably make fewer cognitive switches this way. Importantly, it can feel better to them, even if their measurable performance is worse.

For some people, going faster will mean remembering long enough to forget. This can create the experience for a student of thinking they learned something because it made sense at the time. Panic can occur when the information suddenly seems to be missing, such as when it comes time to write about it or take a test. Students with executive function challenges may:

- Miss or have trouble following directions/forget what to do in their online portal

- Have tantrums about things that appear fairly minor and manageable to you

- Melt down instead of expressing feelings and frustrations about work

- Passively or actively procrastinate by moving from task to task or looking for distractions and doing anything but completing any one task

- Mix up assignments or forget to bring home the resources needed to complete work

- Believe they do not need a system because they intend to do the work

- Struggle to initiate multi-part or less structured assignments such as studying for a test or writing an essay

- Blame the teacher or assessment for being unfair when performance doesn't reflect how hard they think they worked

- Struggle when it comes to using feedback like grades and comments as tools for improvement

Over time, a person needs to develop executive function capacity, not just try to escape the discomfort of its inefficiencies.

Managing the Work Zone

Consider the graph in Figure 5, which shows the relationship of anxiety or boredom to the availability of time. In the *work zone* shown in the middle, the difficulty of a task is well matched for the time available to get it done. To get into the work zone, your child will need to manage both how much time there is to accomplish a task, and how difficult they perceive the task to be. If the difficulty including the number of steps and switches is overwhelming, your child will not start the new task. Being able to find and honor a personal work zone sweet spot for various types of tasks can make learning significantly easier and more rewarding.

Avoidance is one of the most common ways for people with executive function challenges to manage the Stop-Switch-Start process. Avoidance works by increasing the amount of anxiety and decreasing the time available. Then, finally, the student must either do something such as cram for a test or declare it beyond the realm of possibility and seek a worthy distraction.

Figure 5: The Work Zone

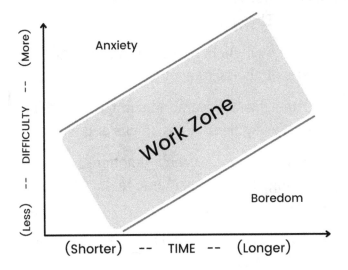

All of us have to work at accurately calibrating our self-awareness skills, especially when it comes to knowing when to heed the call of comforting avoidance versus just getting started. Your child is not really out to make life miserable when they put things off until the last minute. Doing so may give them the energy to get the task done.

Procrastination as an Executive Function Problem

Procrastination is a response to emotions. Not wanting to do something is a feeling, bolstered by the rumbling background noise of a potential emotion storm. This is completely normal. For chronic procrastinators, what is challenging is learning to hear the rumble, sit through the emotion storm, and move on with the work anyway. To review handling emotional storms, go back to Chapter 2.

People procrastinate when they do not have needed skills, including academic skills, executive functions, and emotional self-regulation. They may:

- Become overwhelmed by the number of switches and restarts in an assignment

- Find that tasks become meaningless, tedious, or baffling, causing them to lose focus and energy

- Struggle to regulate their emotions, especially when appealing small transitions might provide potential escapes

- Be worried about possible consequences and wonder, *What if I make a mistake?*

- Not know how to plan steps for what to do next

The result is the *procrastinator's pause*. It's like a rest stop someone just cannot resist on the assignment superhighway. How can someone take advantage of it without having it become a long-term stopover?

Procrastination generally picks up in middle or high school because expectations significantly increase for managing independent work. It can be hard for students to sequence multiple steps and keep track of technology-based communication. You can help your child learn a framework that provides structure, routines, and limits so that creativity, accountability, and home civility thrive in your family. Can you identify the particular aspects of executive functioning that are not working efficiently for your child? See the full chart in Table 9.

Executive Functions Applied

As an adult, you may think that a child's work is fairly simple compared with your adult responsibilities. But children, especially those with the lived experience of learning, attention, or executive function challenges, can find their tasks confusing and overwhelming. The normal thing to do when feeling overwhelmed is make a list and tackle it one step at a time, right? Not if you struggle to engage your Stop-Switch-Start executive functions. Procrastination happens when people struggle at the intersection of self-awareness and self-regulation. *Self-awareness* makes it possible to recognize strong emotional signals about whether to take action or not. *Self-regulation* leads to appropriate action, given the context and requirements.

Before ever getting to work, emotions fueled by background noise send information about whether to engage the Stop-Switch-Start sequence or not. When your child is off track, they may appear distracted and unfocused to you. Because emotions are tricky, your child is likely to be unaware that they are taking action to protect themselves and prevent pain instead of engaging in Stop-Switch-Start. Your child's protection and prevention thoughts are about emotional safety.

These thoughts are like the background noise of an approaching storm, as described in Chapter 2. Your procrastinating child may miss cues from the time when the storm was still approaching, and they may now find themselves lost in a swirl of stormy weather. Whether you can see the storm or not and whether it is fast-moving or stationary, procrastination is your child's attempt to escape it. Your child wants to be in a calmer, more pleasant, and more focused place, away from schoolwork stress.

Your child's procrastination may look to you like anything from passive resistance to a full-on meltdown. But to your child it can feel like rage, terror, or gloom. They think:

- *It's so unfair.*

- *I don't know what to do.*

- *I'll never figure it out.*

These thoughts refuel powerful emotions: Anger. Fear. Sadness. Shame. They make your child feel as if something needs to be done. Escape now! Do not let anyone find out!

Adults can help with well-designed home and classroom accommodations for managing executive functions. These help students regulate their emotional responses to their work by limiting both the number of switches and the working memory required to perform each step. Chapter 9 describes one of my favorite ways to help students manage their work.

Taking Talent Into Consideration: Asher's Story

Like other students you are meeting in this book, Asher struggled to get his work done independently. He was gifted with beauty and physical grace. In middle school, when some of his peers were still developing, Asher appeared at ease, mature, and polished. This was on the outside. His inner executive functioning resources were a mismatch for this bright, attractive young man. By high school Asher came across to adults as sophisticated but careless. They felt he was clearly underperforming. His work seemed rushed; small details were omitted, and directions were missed. This was especially apparent in writing assignments where Asher seemed to bog down. He struggled to get started and then seemed to lose steam after a couple of paragraphs, feeling that he was done before he completed an assignment. *He ought to be able to do better than this*, Asher's parents and teachers thought.

Because he was the youngest of four children, Asher's parents knew that not all children learn or process in the same way. But they also thought of him as generally careless since he forgot so many small life details beyond school. He never seemed to finish things. That is, except races. He raced in a variety of individual sports for his school. In the fall, it was cross country. In the winter, it was downhill skiing. In the spring, it was track. In the summer, it was sailing at camp. He was very good and very fast at all of these sports. Asher loved going fast as well as having enough time in a race to warm up, speed up, and power to the end for the win. While racing required speed, energy, and strategy, it did not seem to require the ability to analyze, synthesize, plan well, or argue a point of view the way writing did.

Planning schoolwork made Asher anxious. It just took too long, considering that the assignment was going to take a long time by itself. Then there would be more assignments. Asher avoided and procrastinated. He made no excuses for what he thought was a logical strategy, even though it was not getting good results. His working memory and attention span were just not long enough.

What Asher did not know about procrastination was that it was tied to his emotional self-regulation. He needed to down-regulate some emotions in order to control impulsivity and to up-regulate others in order to keep his energy high enough to get work done. He needed to employ stepwise thinking and keep his focus on the *finished* line. Unfortunately, he thought of himself the way the adults in his life did: fast but lazy.

When he was a tenth grader, Asher learned from the varsity track coach that there would be too many runners and not enough field athletes for the upcoming season. Would he be willing to be a jumper? It would involve summer training, as well as attending jumping camp. His parents agreed to camp because they were excited by Asher having new challenges.

Broad jumping was a disaster. It involved standing still and springing up and forward. *No and no*, Asher thought. Long jumping was much better. There was the warm up, speed up, and power through that he loved in racing. He was quickly almost as good as other jumpers who had been practicing for a year or more. But pole vaulting? Oh, this was his new sport. Speeded running, launching, struggling over the pole, and the fall to the finish were all exciting. At the beginning, Asher was the fastest over the pole, clearing his height in seconds. But he also cleared at the lowest height for all of camp. What would it take for him to get better?

Asher was very motivated to be his team's pole vaulter for the following season. There would be a long time through the fall and winter seasons to practice and wait for his chance. Unlike racing sports where he felt naturally fast and talented, Asher needed to perform fairly intricate analyses of individual pole-vaulting passes. This meant reviewing videos of both himself and exemplar vaulters, meeting with a coach to receive feedback, and practicing over and over in ways that incrementally shifted his approach technique and bar clearance height. Since a small lapse in attention or confidence could spell disaster, both physical skills and mental strength were required. He needed to be able to plan, monitor, and adjust. He also needed to deepen his understanding of pole vaulting through practice and reflection.

Asher had been using core executive functions to improve his sport. He was not naturally good at pole vaulting, but he was willing to practice at a special camp and take lots of feedback from his coach. He was very proud of his practice strategies and the success they made possible.

Would Asher, I wondered, be willing to use similar strategies to refine his writing? In listening to his story, I knew that he already understood the importance of practicing skills separately from performing in a meet. Sitting down to write an essay and expecting it to flow smoothly without refining his skills was no more likely to result in a win than practicing pole vaulting without a pole. What would make Asher feel less defensive and more in control of his written output? He needed to warm up, speed up, and power through. He needed to build writing skills and executive functions. He agreed.

Smoothing the Path Forward

It is important to understand the mental behaviors of the planning and monitoring/adjusting executive functions. They're often both intricate and invisible. When they work together well, planning behaviors are guided by a student's monitoring and adjustment along the way to completing work.

The interplay between planning and monitoring/adjusting can be experienced differently by the same person doing different tasks. Someone who is creative and has excellent fluid reasoning and pattern recognition, for example, may understand what they want the end result of an assignment to look like. But during the actual performance of activities with many steps, such as problem solving or writing, the same person can feel lost in the task details. In this case, the monitoring/adjusting may break down, overwhelming them while they work. Some attention to both planning and monitoring/adjusting can make a big difference.

Do? What? How? When? An Approach that Supports Planning

The executive function skill *planning* can be supported by helping students learn a way to uncover all parts of an assignment and perceive embedded directions. An approach that I call *Do-What-How-When* can make a big difference, in my experience.

If you wonder why your child makes so-called careless mistakes, this may be part of their challenge. They may need to analyze the directions systematically so that they perceive all the details. For work that is in digital form, students can annotate, highlight, and use the comments feature to record their analysis.

In particular, with this approach, a child marks up an assignment to identify the different elements. They might highlight or circle what they need to DO, underline WHAT they need to do, draw a square box around elements that tell them HOW to do the task, and make a note in their planners or on the assignment for WHEN it is due. Figure 6 below summarizes this.

Figure 6: Do-What-How-When

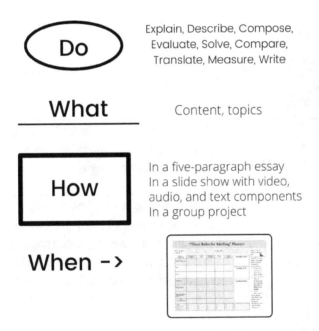

Table 11 shows this approach for three assignments ranging from the simple ones that are often given out in grade school to the complex assignments given out in middle and high school.

The first assignment is very straight-forward. The actual work may not be, but the directions are.

The second assignment is actually several directions. Students may follow the first direction and miss subsequent steps. Before beginning to work, it helps to make these steps more explicit, making it possible to see how many *Do* actions are needed.

The third assignment is even more complex. Now the student must also do the work in a particular way, remember something mentioned in class which they might have missed, and turn it in by a specified time.

Table 11: Examples of Do-What-How-When in Action

	Marked Up Assignment Instructions
Simple (Do = 1, What = 1)	Answer questions 1-5.
Medium (Do = 4, What = 5)	Answer questions 1-5. Show all work. For numbers 3 and 4 explain how you found your answer. Don't forget to check your work!
Complex (Do = 5, What = 5, How = 1, When = 1)	Answer questions 1-5. Show all work. For open-response numbers 3 and 4, explain how you found your answer in a well-organized paragraph. Hint: Remember what we talked about in class. Don't forget to check your work! Due on THURSDAY.

It may be necessary to perform multiple steps to complete a particular task. The more a student understands this, the more likely they are to make *Stop-Switch-Start* and *Monitor/Adjust* moments move smoothly. By helping your child use this approach, you are also helping them develop their own process of learning. They will have clearer ideas about what to assign to themselves, how to check their work, and when they need to ask for help.

What to Do If Your Child's Executive Functions are Uneven

If your child's executive functions need some help and support, look for possible actions in Table 12.

Table 12: Actions to Help Executive Function Development

Approach	Details
Focus on behaviors that do work.	Treat them as strengths, not as context-specific behaviors or preferences. Focus on what is going well even when some things might not be.
Ask children what they think will help.	Review coaching questions in Chapter 4.
Provide previews of coming work.	If transitions are a challenge, limit surprises.
Keep solutions very simple at first so children can do them successfully.	When a solution or strategy works for them with a specific task, ask them how else they could apply it.
If a plan does not work, make the plan even simpler. Break it down and set up for early success.	Moving giraffes is always tricky. What do you have to do? With what content? How is the outcome supposed to look/sound/work? When is it due? Use the Do? What? How? When? approach.
Build in estimation skills from an early age.	Start small. Use a timer. What can be completed in 4, 6, or 10 minutes? Extend the amount of time incrementally. Consider just adding another round of minutes and praising what has been done in that amount of time.
When your child challenges your efforts at helping, ask questions.	Remember how to be your child's coach, as explained in Chapter 4.
Teach children that there are many steps in assignments, and every step has a choice element.	Active choices make you feel more in charge, and they make a measurable improvement in your ability to get things done.

CONCLUSION

Solving complex problems takes more than academic skills. It also requires executive functions that develop over time at different rates in different children. To give your child the gift of making choices that move them forward, appreciate the executive functions that are already solid and support the ones that are still developing.

INKLING 8

Beyond Schoolwork

Executive functions are used in every aspect of life, not just for schoolwork. Think about the last time you went on vacation. Sometimes the amount of apparent effort required to do something you actually want to do can make an otherwise desirable thing very hard to enjoy or learn from before you even get started.

When my children were in middle school, we took them on several trips. They had crossed the border to Canada from the United States, but they had not crossed an ocean. Lured by cheap air fares with a children-fly-free bonus, we chose Ireland for our first international adventure.

We gave the children picture-filled guide books and graphic-novel histories to help them research and contribute their own ideas about what would make the trip fun. They wanted chances to hear and even play along with music at the pubs that let children in. (Remember my son wanted to be in a band.) They wanted to visit ruins older than the pyramids, and they found places mentioned in ancient arts and literature. (My daughter went on to major in Film and History.) They were interested in the great outdoors and exploring quaint shops. They were excited about having foreign currency to spend.

Planning for the trip made us aware of worthy challenges for adults, too: dual-language signage, paper maps, and a different place to stay each night for over a week. To reach them? We'd need to drive a standard-shift car on the left and in the dark. I was responsible for managing the overall trip design and plugging in the places everyone wanted to visit. We worked out a self-guided driving route for maximum geographic coverage. The children used a giant paper map and highlighters to help plan the trip routes and attractions.

We skipped hotels in favor of simple accommodations in guest houses throughout Ireland. Local charm! Adventure! The children wanted to stay in a castle, so we found one. We made packing lists and shopping lists. Anything that would not make it into a suitcase or backpack, we'd have to do without. Since we would be moving our giraffes from location to location, we did last-minute unpacking to keep the load light and limited to essentials.

When There is No Escaping Stormy Weather

The day we left, it was February in New England. A storm-of-the-century blizzard was forecast to arrive just as we were flying out. Snowflakes flew furiously around us while our aircraft was deiced. We took off in the snow and made it safely to the warmth and green grass of Ireland. Each night we planned to drive to a new location, to awake each morning in a place we had only read about at home. We had planned a charming adventure.

Sometimes planning and organization are considered the most important parts of executive functions. An outside observer often thinks that better time and materials management can prevent problems. We had planned very carefully based on thorough research. February was typically a dry month in otherwise rainy Ireland. It was supposed to be warm compared to Boston. However, the evening we arrived, Dublin was facing its largest snowfall in 50 years. They had no plows or snow shovels. We had no winter hats, gloves, or boots.

Our charming 1780s-era accommodation, while within walking distance of everything we wanted to see, had a window pane missing. Snow blew into the one frigid room we shared. There was no one to fix it for us since they were presumably trying to keep warm somewhere else. We slept in our clothes. In the morning there was no hot water. All we wanted was to be warm. Unfortunately, to do that we would have to go out into the very cold and very wet city to find a heated place. We would have to keep moving our luggage along snowy sidewalks, like so many little giraffes.

....
Learn to Plan, Do, and Adjust

This chapter introduces an effective technique for breaking complex directions into manageable parts. The *Three Rules for Adulting* can help a child behave more and more like a responsible adult. Children become more independent by assigning work to themselves, actively seeking a variety of feedback beyond grades, and making adjustments based on the feedback.

With these rules, executive functions meet time management. Using them, your child can make effective *choices* about the way they approach work, which together with *competence*, form the foundation for the third gift, *self-direction*, which will be described in Chapters 10 and 11.

Rule Overview

Rule number one is to assign yourself the time and kind of work. It's called *Time and Kind* for short.

The second rule, *Seek Feedback*, is to identify a variety of data points, including but not limited to grades, in order to know what is working well and where changes are needed. Rather than waiting for grades at the end of the term, the student who seeks feedback collects information every day so they can make incremental adjustments.

The third rule, *Make Adjustments*, is to apply the knowledge gained from feedback to make incremental changes in the way they perform work. While making adjustments, students often assign new time and kind to themselves.

Together, the Three Rules for Adulting is an ongoing cycle as shown in Figure 7.

Figure 7: The Three Rules for Adulting

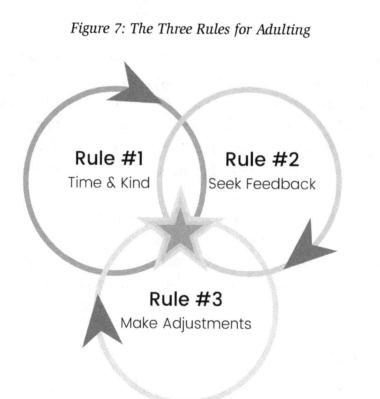

Just Try? Introduction to Owen

One of my students, Owen, did a masterful job of applying these three practices and then reflecting on the difference they made for him. In the rest of this chapter, we will explore each rule and then illustrate it with the journal entries that Owen made while he was reflecting on the difference the rules made in his life.

But first, let's look at Owen's experience before the rules were put in place.

"Listen, buddy," the science teacher, Mr. Sanchez, said to 14-year-old Owen. "You've got to pull up those grades. I need you to do the work. You've got it in you. Hey, I heard you're even in the million-dollar seat now in every class – right up front. Just try, ok?"

Teachers always acted as if they believed that any temporary progress was evidence that Owen was turning it around. Whatever "it" was. But Owen felt deeply ashamed that so many enthusiastic well-meaning adults had become endlessly disappointed in him. His parents teased that they had given him the right name, "Oh, when." He had long-since come to believe that he was not much of a student, and that learning was something that he did for others, not for himself. Whenever they nudged him, Owen did what he could until the momentum wore off.

It had become increasingly difficult to even want to try harder. The likelihood of disappointing the adults in his life was getting higher as he got older. Maybe it would be better to go out not swinging. His baseball coach said he should never do that: "Always take the chance that the next time could be great." Or, Owen imagined, fly out on a pop foul, right to the catcher.

At the beginning of the second semester of tenth grade, teachers sat Owen down and offered him goal-setting instruction to keep him on the curriculum superhighway toward college. He said that yes, he did plan to apply to college in the future and yes, he intended to turn in his work this semester to support that goal. Everyone agreed that Owen had the ability to reach this goal, and that it could happen over the course of the spring semester. Except it did not work out that way. Bad study habits. Forgetfulness. Poor planning. Digital distractions. Moodiness. There were many potential reasons why his goals were not being met.

Owen was so far behind. His school kept offering him short-term executive function interventions and general education support to improve his grades. Sometimes those bits of help gave him a temporary boost. All of the teachers seemed to think he could do the work. But to Owen, schoolwork was a painful reminder of his multitude of failures.

We will come back to Owen after the explanation of each rule.

Rule #1: Assign Time and Kind

You may have already seen that your older child is more motivated to do their assignments when they consider them their own work rather than an imposition by someone else. This is especially true of adolescents.

You will know this is happening when you hear your child say, "I have a science assignment to complete," instead of saying, "I have Mr. Grayson's homework." You may also hear your child independently prioritizing assignments before entertainment or socializing. It can sound like this: "Hey, I'm done with all of my homework and ahead on my reading. I'd like to go to the basketball game tonight. Is that ok?" This is when you know that your child is using the first rule for adulting.

Taking ownership of responsibilities is an important part of being an adult. The teacher has already done their part by creating the assignment. To come up with their assignments, teachers think like this, in terms of curriculum and purpose-driven questions:

- *What standards will the students be able to meet as a result of the activities in a given unit or lesson?*

- *What skills will be needed, applied, or learned?*

- *How long will I have to cover this content with students?*

- *What activities are optimal for student learning in this time frame?*

- *What questions will drive student learning?*

- *What assignments will I give to support this learning?*

- *How will I assess what has been learned?*

Students tend to think in more practical questions. They might not typically plan past the end of a day and instead rely on memory or a quick portal check.

- *Is there an assignment?*

- *Do I have to do it?*

- *Is it due tomorrow?*

You might think that this forward-thinking, "What do I have to do?" approach would be effective for completing assignments. But students who are getting their work done and turned in on time are not using this reactive method. Their success may be because they already have excellent executive function skills.

The following are fundamental skills of Rule #1: Assign the Time and Kind of the Work.

1. Recording the *when* and *what* of work to be done, in a planner or calendar, virtual or paper

2. Planning ahead with the end in mind, working backwards from the desired end

3. Breaking down large tasks into practical actionable steps

4. Estimating time and prioritizing activities

Using a Planner to Prioritize

Parents often wish their child were better at prioritizing. It is easier to prioritize when all of the possible work is structured in writing for today as well as the week ahead. Homework planners are usually provided during the later elementary grades when students are beginning to be assigned more homework. Teachers tell students what to write in the boxes on each page, but then two things happen that actually discourage the use of a planner or calendar.

First, it is no longer required to use a planner in middle school, despite the fact that there is more homework and there are even more teachers assigning it since all subjects are now taught separately. Second, middle and high school teachers use a variety of online resources. They post their assignments and due dates to classroom management systems that can populate due dates to calendars automatically. However, having the work posted automatically for them is not a way to teach your child the essential abilities of prioritizing and working backwards.

Fortunately, there is no need to waste precious working memory trying to memorize something that belongs in a structured calendar or planner. I have used the structured calendar approach demonstrated in Figure 8 extensively with students in my practice. This approach can be implemented with a paper calendar, such as a teacher plan book, or integrated into an online calendar such as Google, iCal, or Outlook. Using this approach enables any planner to guide student planning more effectively.

First, notice that it is not enough to enter when something is due. In the first example, English, the student using this calendar finds out on Monday that a paper is due on Thursday. The student extends the assignment backwards from the future due date (Thursday 3/27) to the present (Monday 3/24). This assignment occupies a spot in every day in this series, not just on the due date or the day before. The bottom corner of the Thursday block for English is colored in with a triangle so that it stands out as the due date whenever the calendar is consulted. Note that the representation of this writing assignment would be even better if the student had broken it up into smaller parts rather than simply listing "Paper Due" in each slot.

Figure 8: Structured Calendar to Support Three Rules for Adulting

THREE RULES FOR ADULTING						
Week of... 3/24-3/30	Mon 3/24	Tues 3/25	Wed 3/26	Thu 3/27 1/2 day. Yay!	Fri 3/28	
English/ Language Arts	Paper due Thursday	Paper due Thursday	Paper due Thursday	Paper due		**Sat** **3/29** Soccer 4:30
Math	Test Friday Practice problems	Test Friday Ex Help	Test Friday Make practice test	Test Friday Take practice test	Test	**Sun** **3/30**
Science		Lab			Lab due	
Social Studies	Review Notes/ Compare to Book	Quiz Thu?	Quiz tomorrow?	Quiz		
Foreign Language	Quiz Wed LangLab after school	Quiz Wed Practice with Joe	Oral Quiz			
Art/Music/ Specials A.W.E. (And What Else?)		Bring batteries for tomorrow				
After School Activities	LangLab, Game	Ex Help		Game		
WWW 1. What went well? 2. What was good about it? 3. How can I get more?	1. 2. 3.	1. 2. 3.	1. 2. 3.	1. 2. 3.	1. 2. 3.	1. 2. 3.

Notes
- SS test 83 (prac test)
- Sci quiz 3/5 (pop quiz, did not study)
- Lyrics distract when writing
- Check for all steps in directions

Work Backwards
What is the goal? What steps are needed to accomplish it?
1. **Assign time and day and the kind** of work needed.
2. **Seek Feedback**: Record performance and what got you there in Notes and in WWW.
3. **Make Adjustments**: Start sooner / Break into parts / Do. What. How. When? with directions / Ask for help / What else?

For the second example, Math, the test is on Friday. This is mentioned by the teacher in class on Monday, and the student has extended the assignment backwards. Notice also that the student has assigned strategies for each day leading up to the test. These might take just five minutes each day. Every student to whom I have shown this example agrees that they would be very likely to both learn more and improve their test performance if they tried these small choices.

The bottom of this planner also has a place to keep track of what has been going well each day. Even writing down one thing each day that did go well means choosing to pay attention to a win. While it might be random (fire drills happen), chances are that the good thing has something to do with a student action (reached out to a friend; teacher showed my project as a good example). By writing down the good things, students are giving themselves feedback that can become the basis of future strategies.

Below the structured calendar, notice that the rules are explained in brief, along with reminders of effective techniques such as the *Do-What-How-When* approach explained in Chapter 8.

There is a box for specific feedback and notes to self about possible adjustments, which we will discuss with Rules #2 and #3. There are also spots for weekend assignments.

While it may look like a lot more needs to be done in a week this way, it is more efficient and more effective to visualize and record all of the things to do in one place, prioritize by making choices about them, and work on smaller bits. The goal is to continue to assign the work to be done, seeing it in the context of a time frame of at least a week.

Parents can help their children learn to prioritize by asking questions. Use your parent coaching skills here. For students who struggle to start tasks, ask which is the smallest possible thing to do on a given day. Your child can write #1 in the box for that day's assignment and do it first. Do not suggest they start with the hardest or longest thing because that is the recipe for discouragement for anyone struggling to start tasks.

Then ask what they think would be a good next step. They can mark it #2. Then they can choose another short thing, and follow it up with a longer or more challenging assignment. Continue in this way with small steps. You are helping your child to build up their sense of accomplishment by having the experience of completing tasks. This makes parents happier, too! It is a valuable lifelong skill to be able to break up longer tasks that seem overwhelming into a series of smaller ones.

What About Breaks?

Here is an important reminder. Breaks can be helpful resets, but they also can provide attractive distractions and challenging restarts. If you are wondering about your child taking breaks, help them to make a "start here" mini-direction for themselves. For example, it could be a comment in their writing assignment, a circled number of the next problem in a math or science set, or a browser tab for an online flashcard study site. Have them cue up the reminder about where to resume before stepping away. Then your child will know where to start when they return.

Rule #1 Involves Planning and Skill-building

It is unfortunate that many students believe that planning is synonymous with extra work rather than being a time-saver that helps them streamline their work and visualize its outcome. Written planning can be a tough sell for children who can manage and remember their work early in their student careers. So can decoding unfamiliar words, learning how to write a complete sentence, or practicing the times tables, but you would never say those are unimportant skills.

> *An actively created calendar/planner can reduce the amount of executive function power required for work. This frees up brain power for more learning, the true goal of education. On the larger scale of planning, learning to envision their lives beyond what other people plan for them today is as fundamental to student success as knowing how to read, write, and solve problems.*

Part of assigning time and kind to themselves involves understanding how to learn skills. This can be different for each person. Each student has to discover their own unique recipe for learning, usually through trial and error, feedback, and adjustment. Incidental learning that occurs by just doing assignments is not enough. Students who learn efficiently use abstract thinking and action tactics so that learning and studying are directly linked. This makes it easier for them to learn new information and retrieve it when relevant for the rest of their lives.

Rule #1 in Action: Owen Assigns Time and Kind

"Owen," the teacher's raised voice popped into his awareness. "Buddy, I'm just here doing my job. Giving you the assignments. Grading the work. Keeping you on track to finish out the term strong." Owen could feel himself checking out again. His cheeks and chest felt hot now. He did not really know how much work he needed to do because he hadn't written any of it down. Instead, because work was listed online, Owen used a reactive rather than proactive approach to knowing about his assignments. Thus, he was never in charge of his time or his responsibilities. Assignments, even the ones connected clearly to his big goals, felt like impositions. The reactive approach meant staying up late for important last-minute assignments, feeling dozy in class the next day, missing important details during class, and feeling embarrassed when called upon.

It took more than a semester for Owen to master the first rule, *Time and Kind*, with any regularity. That's because he relied on having other people assign tasks for him. For Owen to be successful at meeting his goals, he needed to assign work to himself and plan the steps to get it done.

Here is how Owen turned it around. It was not easy, and he pushed back a lot during the first three months. By the end of the semester, though, Owen had learned not just how to follow the rules but why he wanted to stick with them. The comments in Figure 9 are adapted from Owen's reflection journal composed at the end of the school year.

Figure 9: Rule #1: Owen Masters Assigning Time and Kind

Rule #1: Assign Time and Kind

What I used to do:
- No calendar or planner/Looked online to see if anything was due the next day only
- Worked through the week without a schedule or plan for how to complete schoolwork
- Waited for the last minute before the due date/time to do schoolwork
- Saved my schoolwork for the end of the day, late at night
- Stayed up late to finish, fell asleep, or abandoned things altogether
- Avoided everything. Tried to sleep in, even on school days

What I do now:
- Use my online calendar to assign myself the time and kind of work
- Use calendar app for phone
- Set it up at the beginning of the week, including all times when I will be in school or otherwise not available for doing homework
- Use repeat feature so even though I check Mondays and daily, I only have to set up most of it one time, at the beginning of the semester
- See how much of my time is available for work or anything, really, instead of just looking to see if I have any assignments
- Export assignments to my calendar from the school's system but understand that some teachers do not use the system
- Realize that I was always hoping for there to be no work. This is a big shift, to focus on open time so I can use it productively
- Make the workday shorter: Leave as much time in the evening as free as possible to do my work more productively during the daytime and shorten my working hours
- See the amount of time I use productively compared to how much time I waste
- Enjoy myself more in general, not let the schedule be in charge of me
- Sleep better
- Socialize more

Hardest part:
- Believing it would help
- Thinking all the set up would be worth it
- Making it a habit (which took most of the semester)

Most important part:
- Make the last minute happen sooner
- Set an earlier deadline (a day or so ahead)
- It's all the rules together

Rule #2: Seek Feedback

Whatever system a person may be using, they will usually stick with it until it doesn't work. Feedback is how we discover what is working and what is not. Feedback can come in many forms.

Let's look at this in the context of buying food to meet your needs or those of your family.

One kind of feedback might let you know if you have been purchasing the right kinds, sizes, and amounts of different foods. As long as you feel pretty confident in your system and how it works for you, it can become a useful routine. Each time you open the fridge and find that the things you need are there, you're getting the feedback that your system is working. All you need to do is assign yourself the same time and general work for the next shopping trip. There may be unexpected stressors such as someone unexpectedly eating what you planned to serve for dinner, but you can have a contingency plan such as ordering take-out.

Other people in your family may not agree with your food choices or appreciate your cooking. That's feedback, too. You may be very flexible about meeting other people's needs and be eager to please them. On the other hand, you might find this food feedback hurtful and discouraging. After all, you work hard all day and you just want a pleasant meal with your family. It's not as if the food is bad. It's just not exactly what they want right now. Based on this feedback, you can make choices. Should you choose to do things the same way, keeping your system and expecting others to adjust to it? Or should you choose to try something new?

In a similar way, every student needs to learn to evaluate their own work products and not just depend on someone else to say what is good about them. Well into higher education, rubrics are provided so that students can evaluate their work according to teacher standards. But students also need to be able to evaluate the quality of resources and information for their own use. Evaluating their own work includes editing, checking work, and seeking feedback from others. Ideally, students move past working just to increase grades. They also evaluate what they are learning. They stop seeing every outcome as being random and start understanding that their choices make a difference. Look at the Notes box in Figure 8 on page page 182 to see an example of the kind of feedback students can give themselves.

Rule #2 in Action: Owen Seeks Feedback and Reflects on Progress

Owen started his journal entries by describing what he used to do. When he reviewed them later, he found them full of feedback. These journal entries helped him see what was not working well and suggested ways he could make different choices with his time. Figure 10 shows what Owen observed about his progress with Rule #2. While it might have been easy to focus only on what needed to be fixed, I wanted Owen to know that at least some parts of any system are already effective.

Figure 10: Rule #2: Owen Masters Seeking Feedback

Rule #2: Seek Feedback

What I used to do:
- If an assignment had been turned in or just forgotten about, I moved on
- Relied on teachers to cut me slack so I would not have to face up to my failures
- Took all feedback as criticism, not help
- Directed anger at teachers and my parents

What I do now:
- Figure out what is in my control
- See the work as part of my life
- Go to extra help sessions
- Seek feedback from teachers (I even email them now) to improve/know what to keep doing
- Keep track of my study approaches and what works
- I could not have believed it at the beginning, but this actually saves me time

Rule #3: Make Adjustments

Part of helping students with Rule #3, *Make Adjustments,* is guiding students to come up with their own potential solutions. They can make adjustments, try these out for a period of time, preferably without adult cueing or nagging, and evaluate them for success. If the adjustments work, students can feel the pride that comes with solving their own problems. If the solutions need tweaking, that's just part of making adjustments. Here are three approaches my students often use:

1. **Take choices away:** One way to keep a wandering mind on task is to take choices away. This is not a punishment. Instead, students can make choices in advance to reduce the number and types of choices that need to be made while working on an assignment.

2. **Preemptive planning:** This helps make the last minute happen sooner. That's what a student does when they pack their bag and lay out their clothes the night before. Instead of waiting to realize that they forgot to use the restroom, get their snack, or collect their noise-cancelling headphones, those become part of preemptive planning. With homework, these things happen before students begin an assignment.

3. **If-Then planning:** A child takes a behavior they want to change and shapes it into a new behavior. This involves first identifying the behavior to be changed and then coming up with a practical replacement behavior that your child finds worth assigning to themselves. Here are some examples of behaviors to be replaced; you can imagine replacements:

   » If I just can't focus, then I will _____

   » If I am hungry, then I will _____

   » If I am distracted by my text message chime, then I will_____

   » If I am thinking, *Why bother doing this?* then I will

   _____

   » If I don't know how to do something myself, then I will _____

Rule #3 in Action: Owen Makes Adjustments and Reflects on Progress

Owen learned that the only way to know how things could be different was to experiment by making adjustments and collecting data.

Owen also reflected on how he had learned to make adjustments based on the feedback he received. His journal entries are shown in Figure 11.

Figure 11: Rule #3: Owen Masters Making Adjustments

Rule #3: Make Adjustments

What I used to do:
- Left open tabs, windows, and distractions online while doing schoolwork
- Listened to music or podcasts while doing other work. Answered texts. Thought this was making me happier and keeping me focused but it was the opposite
- Avoided/did the same things that did not help
- Did the opposite of what was asked

What I do now:
- Reduce distractions
- Create work windows only on my computer
- Quit applications I am not using for current work
- Use distractions only during scheduled time
- Experiment with different ways to do better work with less effort
- Keep track of what works for different types of assignments
- Apply what works in multiple classes

My Wins:
- I caught up in classes. No missed work for past month
- Can use this system next semester
- Proud of my work
- Parents and teachers off my case
- Changes where I can look to attend college

Takeaways:
- I have one life, so everything on one calendar
- I plan most effectively by working backwards and practicing time estimation skills
- It can be worth re-trying strategies that have worked well in more than one class
- For continued improvement I should keep doing what works
- I can set goals for myself (either small or large) and test various other strategies to find the ones that work.

Owen's Turn-around

For Owen, trying harder wasn't a long-term solution. As long as he lived in hope that there would be days without assignments, he focused on relief from work rather than pride in doing a good job.

Owen turned this around with coaching that emphasized what was working from his point of view, rather than focusing on what he needed to fix to get better. He also learned about ways to streamline his learning and become more efficient. This made school more interesting, which was far more rewarding than just getting adults to be pleased with him. He was doing the work that was assigned to him, but he was learning for himself. When he applied to college, his personal essay was about his experience of the three rules.

Adjusting Behavior to Move from Procrastinator to Producer: Justina's Story

Parents complain to me about many aspects of raising their children, but a top challenge is the child who does not seem to be able to manage mornings. When I met Justina and her blended family headed by her father and stepmother, Justina was fifteen and attending a private girls' high school. There were smaller classes and more teacher attention than at her old school. Her parents had hoped this school would be the solution to Justina's procrastination. Mornings were the worst; they regularly sounded like this. *Justina's thoughts are in italics.*

"Justina! Are you up yet?"

"I accidentally slept through the alarm."

"Justina! Get dressed!"

"Working on it. Where's my uniform? You didn't wash it?"
"Justina! "You need breakfast. Take this muffin.
"I'm not hungry."
"Justina! We need to leave! We're going to be late!"
"I can't find my backpack."

Justina's parents asked themselves, "Why doesn't she just do what we ask? Why doesn't she just do her homework right when she gets home? Why doesn't she just pack up her book-bag the night before? Why doesn't she get out the door on time? Why doesn't she ask us to proofread her work? Why doesn't she start studying sooner? Why doesn't she go see the teacher for extra help?" They characterized Justina's inaction as misbehavior directed at them.

Justina wanted to improve. She was generally eager to please but lacked strategies. She used two words you will want to listen for, *promise* and *probably,* to describe her intentions for managing her mornings as well as for doing her assigned work. Her statements sounded like this:

- "I *promise* I'll get up on time tomorrow."

- "I'll *probably* get to it tonight."

- "I'll *probably* finish it later."

Your child can learn to listen for the words *probably* and *promise* with your gentle help and replace the related statements with targeted plans that are more productive.

Justina evaluated her own morning struggles and came up with five adjustment experiments. Here are Justina's own set of If-Then starters:

- If I sleep through the alarm, then I will _____
- If I cannot find my backpack, then I will _____
- If I cannot find a clean uniform, then I will _____
- If I don't have time for breakfast, then I will _____
- If I am late to school, then I will _____

Justina noticed that all of her potential solutions involved making the last minute happen sooner. She defined actions that involved getting ready before bedtime. She packed her backpack, laid out her uniform, and even prepared her breakfast the night before. She started the day more regularly on time. She even started feeling excited to get up when she heard the alarm.

Applying the Rules

Table 13 shows what your child needs to be asking and then doing, for every assignment. This summarizes the application of the three rules for adulting, which students can learn to do over and over again for the rest of their lives.

*Table 13: Questions and Actions for Implementing
the Three Rules for Adulting*

Rule	Ask myself	Do
Rule #1: Assign time and kind of work to do	What is the goal? What steps are needed to accomplish it? When will I do it?	Put answers into plan. Stop-Switch-Start. Do the work. Self-monitor, complete, save. Turn it in.
Rule #2: Seek feedback	What techniques went well? Besides grades, what is good about this? What specific efforts made it happen? How can I get a result that is at least that good next time?	Record measured performance and what behaviors got me this result. Take note of even my small wins.
Rule #3: Make adjustments	What did I learn from feedback? How can I celebrate small wins? What changes need to be made? What help do I need?	Reassign myself time and kind, making tweaks based on feedback. Make changes. Manage background noise. Reduce number of choices. Stop-Switch-Start again.

CONCLUSION

The Three Rules for Adulting is a cycle that will be useful for the rest of a student's life. First, students assign work to themselves, keeping track of what needs to be done for a day as well as over extended time periods. Next, students collect feedback, remembering that it can come from sources besides grades. Then, students use feedback information to become more successful by noting what went well and choosing to make small adjustments. The cycle begins again when they assign the small adjustments to themselves. When a student thinks of all learning as iterative, school is an opportunity for discovery and improvement.

INKLING 9

All Learning is Iterative

Like many other adults, I started feeling ambivalent about work in my mid-forties. Figuring out what to do required lots of self-exploration. It was time to design a new career.

Designing anything is not a linear process. *Design thinking* is a way to imagine, prototype, and test something new. During the imagination stage, the designer needs to understand the needs of the end user. The designer of my new career was me, and I needed to figure out who were my end users. Next came generating possible ideas and choosing one to try out or prototype. Then came testing. I collected feedback, made adjustments, and tried again. Each iteration of the prototype design is an opportunity to learn and make the design even better for the end user.

I assigned myself the time and kind of work to get started on my self-design journey. This part was easy for me. I found a career coaching program, answered their introductory questions, and took tests that assessed my strengths, interests, values, and personality. I was so excited to receive the results and discover the next iteration of my work. What new things would I be learning? Would I be going back to school?

My career testing did not result in a list of perfect jobs or careers. I needed to sift through all of the data those assessments generated. That was me seeking feedback. I already knew that not all feedback is provided as numerical metrics. It was frustrating to go through data that included very few yes-or-no answers, particularly since different findings seemed to contradict each other.

I used *design thinking* to treat each idea that emerged as a possible version of better. Design thinking starts with empathy for end user needs, then moves through initial designs, prototyping, collecting feedback from end users, and making improvements based on their responses.

What helped me the most was getting feedback from students and their parents. I decided that they were the end users of my work. Every adjustment I made was done to make things work better for them. This is called *human-centered design*. Collecting feedback and making adjustments continues in my work to this day.

Not having to choose an end game was very liberating. It took away a lot of the need to be right or perfect before moving ahead. As I have told many students over the years, I value improvement over perfection.

CHAPTER 10

Uncover Strengths

Strengths show up in many ways in school, including ways that can look like barriers to success. Helping students discover strengths beyond academic skills is an important part of helping them successfully achieve complex goals on their own terms. The strengths that are most valued in school may blind us to other strengths. Supporting your child's strengths across contexts can be essential to them discovering their future story for college and career success.

What is a Strength?

Think of strengths as positive behaviors that come relatively easily to your child and help them build understanding, see patterns, and get a job done effectively. Once identified, these strengths can be used for future challenges.

It can be hard to work against one's strengths. Remember that they are behaviors on self-drive that often feel right. So honest people can find it hard to tell a white lie, and forgiving people may let others hurt them over and over.

Any time you react with strong negative emotion and think judgmental thoughts, it is worth asking yourself if a strengths button has been pushed, that is, whether you feel that a strength has been violated. Since your relationships with others at home, at your child's school, and at work depend on balancing your needs and wants with theirs, knowing how to manage tense moments can give you the ability to slow things down (see Chapter 2), ask before you tell (see Chapter 4), and find the strengths behind your own reactions.

Strengths Spotting

Spotting student strengths supports learning approaches and strategies that lead to success. When you talk with your child about their strengths, use specific language to describe ways that you have seen your child use them, not just that they have strong math or English grades. That way you can reinforce particular efforts that have worked for your child rather than requiring that they be good at every strategy and strength.

When you ask questions about strengths, student-generated answers can help them to establish consistent structure and flexible systems. Support their strengths-based efforts, helping your child see how their own learning approaches work for them.

The statements in Table 14 are examples of comments you might make to your child when you spot strengths in action. Notice that most start with "I notice." That reinforces that you perceive their strengths coming from them, not being imposed from outside. These statements can open a conversation about their strengths.

Table 14: Strengths-spotting Comments and Questions

Situation	What you might say
Things are going well in school. This is an opportunity to show what you notice and help your student see the strengths they are using.	"I notice that you are doing well on all of your quizzes and tests. I see you persisting even when things are difficult. What other strengths are you using?"
You notice strengths showing up in contexts outside school that could also be useful in school situations. Your comments and questions can help your student see that they could redirect a strength such as curiosity.	"I notice that you are able to answer every question I ask you about major league baseball. How do you do that? You must be really curious, and you must have found a great way to organize the information in your head. What else would you like to learn like that?"
Collaborating and working well with others are also important strengths for learning. Help your student see what they contribute to the group and how they benefit from the strengths of others.	"I notice that you and your friend did something together that surprised both of you. How did you work together to get such a good result? What was it like working together?"
Your child seems unusually excited about going to school. You think you know why, but you check in to make sure you have it right.	"I notice that you were really excited to go to school today. Was it because you were making your presentation today? How did it go? What went well?"
Help them see that the strengths they use in school can be important as they move on to college and work.	"You have really managed a lot this year. I am proud of the way you kept up with all your courses and activities. I know it took a lot of planning and strategic attention."

Character Strengths Affect School Performance

Table 15 shows how some strengths that are not explicitly part of the school curriculum can be associated with school achievement.

Table 15: Character Strengths Affecting School Achievement

Strength	Positive Student Example
Self-regulation	Applies self-awareness and self-control in learning and social situations
Curiosity	Sustains interest in school curriculum topics. Independently seeks additional information
Optimism	Expects good outcomes from efforts, reinforcing desire to try
Enthusiasm	Shows energy and eagerness for learning and schoolwork
Persistence	Perseveres. Maintains purposeful goal-directed behaviors
Gratitude	Is appreciative of opportunities and others' efforts
Social give-and-take	Knows how to work well with other members of teams. Helps others with their learning. Asks for help when needed

Trying On Strengths

The first time a student meets with me, I am eager to discover what they think is best about themselves. Before that initial meeting, I have usually received lots of information about them from teachers, parents, and testers. The documentation tells me about diagnoses, interventions, treatments, struggles over time, current struggles, fears for the future, and what has not worked. Sadly, but understandably, when I ask questions about what is best about them, students generally respond, "I don't know. No one has ever asked me that before."

Nearly every student also says, "I guess you could say I'm nice."

The rest of that first session is devoted to uncovering at least some of what the student likes about themselves. A bit at a time, they then learn to see ways in which what they enjoy about themselves and what they are proud of can be valuable tools for learning.

I help students uncover ways they are already using a strength. Then I coach them to think of new ways to use it. This approach is more motivating in the short term and more powerful in the long run than continually trying to fix what is wrong with them.

You may wonder how being nice can be useful if you are struggling in Algebra. That will depend on what the student means by nice. Nice can mean agreeable, pleasant, friendly, good-natured, and likable. Some opposites of nice are unfriendly, unpleasant, disagreeable, unattractive, and unappealing. In Chapter 6, when Kai made teachers think she cared, she was applying her strength of being nice to self-advocacy and getting help. Teachers were generally eager to help her, and this motivated Kai to continue requesting help.

In Chapter 7, Nikhil did not find it easy to tap this strength. Many teachers found him disengaged, impulsive, and disinterested in schoolwork. Seeing him as bright but not really trying, they attributed his lack of success in the curriculum to his own poor behavior. When I asked what was best about him, Nikhil did not say that nice was his best trait. He proudly said what was best about him was honesty and knowing when not to waste time. He was a tough critical thinker who sized up situations and people quickly. It was hard for him to reconsider a decision once it had been made. He needed to be encouraged to imagine his future including some flexibility. He also needed to see that knowing how to learn could be valuable, even if the actual content of schoolwork seemed irrelevant to him in the present.

Strengths are often valuable character traits that encompass both skills and personality.   Here are some ways they show up in school reports and teacher comments:

- "Jazmyn is calm, gives good advice, and learns math quickly."

- "Sevi is good at chemistry and fair on the playing field."

- "Alana is kind, creative, persistent, funny, and grateful."

Learning to appreciate strengths can involve looking at behaviors in new ways. I have seen parents struggle to value in their children the behaviors that they really admire in other adults. For example, this may mean shifting your viewpoint to appreciate the way your child sticks up for themselves or expresses strong opinions.

Some Strengths Blind Us to Others: My Daughter at Odds with School

Some strengths are valued in some contexts but not in others. Strengths can even seem like behavior problems or disabilities. When my daughter was in middle school, her English teacher called to tell me how very concerned she was about my daughter's distractibility. "Do you know how very challenging it is to teach your daughter anything?" This teacher sounded exasperated. But her complaint did not add up to me.

"Thank you for calling. Can you tell me more about this?" I answered in my best neutral voice while trying to check in with my background noise. From my point of view, my daughter was a curious and eager learner. At any given time, she might be reading about reptiles, fantasy literature, historical fiction, babysitting skills, and animation art, but she could keep the threads straight. She illustrated the books as she went along. She sang in three choirs, and she was the catcher on her softball team. She did quite well at school despite finding it rather boring since she felt there was not much new content to learn. Challenging to teach this eager learner? How could that be true?

The teacher continued by offering evidence for her challenging-to-teach verdict. "Your daughter doodles when I am speaking or when she is in a group. Then she races through her work, takes a book from her backpack, and reads for most of the class. I have caught her reading ahead in the novel I am teaching in class when I explicitly asked for no one to do this. I often have to call on her to be sure she is paying attention."

While the teacher was talking, I pulled out the four-inch binder with my daughter's name on it where I kept printouts of her school documents. The most recent report card showed an A grade in this class. So at least she was doing her work and passing the assessments.

I asked, "I am a bit confused. Can you say what seems to be the problem?"

"Ms. Fisher, your daughter is very capable, but she is not even trying to pay attention in my class. She does not seem to care about learning."

I hope you noticed the teacher's background noise. Her thoughts and beliefs about what it meant to be a learner did not seem to lean toward curiosity and creativity. Instead, she believed strengths like focus and conformity were necessary for learning to occur in her students. What's more, she felt she deserved gratitude for the effort it required to keep cueing my distractible daughter's attention.

On the one hand I appreciated that the teacher saw my daughter's potential, labeling her "very capable" in our conversation. On the other hand, I felt that the teacher needed different tools for tapping my daughter's learning strengths.

Strengths Favored in School

In the K-12 school context, adults can become frustrated with students they think need to show more of certain strengths, especially if a student appears to have the intelligence to do the work of the curriculum but is somehow struggling. If only they tried harder. This thought story can make it easy to see the lack of certain strengths as a weakness, even though there may be other strengths in there that could be appreciated. What is also true? How is the student's behavior based on strengths that may not be as clearly valued in schools?

School learning is not typically tailored to all kinds of student strengths. Instead, students who bring the already-valued school strengths shown in Table 15 on page page 202 have an edge over their classmates who have other strengths such as high energy, a sense of humor, bravery, honesty, and creativity. A child with favored strengths may appear studious and focused, while a child with other strengths may seem like a born entertainer at the expense of learning the curriculum.

Strengths Not So Valued in School: Ramesh's Humor

Of course, any strength can be used inappropriately or to an extreme. Take humor, for example. Ramesh loved to delight other people. When he was a preschooler, he was the one who could make babies stop crying and belly laugh instead. When he began school, this strength was endearing. He amused his classmates by adopting different voices for characters when he read aloud. He was a natural for spoiler parts in school plays. But Ramesh's humor strength was not well-suited for classroom learning in later grades.

Knowing Personal Strengths and Using a Volume Slider

Knowing one's own strengths and having a language for them can create a powerful sense of self that buffers against school's ups and downs. Loud and disrespectful are undesirable labels. But Ramesh thought of himself as nice and funny.

Imagine thinking, as Ramesh learned to do, that you have the strength of enthusiasm that comes with a volume slider. It is not that you are loud and disrespectful. You just have your enthusiasm up too high for the situation. That means you can slide it down, too.

Even the strengths that are most valued in school can be expressed with too much or too little vigor. Here are ways that valued strengths might need to be dialed back:

- Overuse of enthusiasm for learning more and curiosity may keep a child from moving on to the next topic when the teacher is ready to move on.

- Overuse of perseverance through challenges may look like perfectionism that keeps a child from turning in work on time.

- Overuse of optimism might blind a child to feedback so that they do not see the benefit of trying an alternative approach.

- Overuse of social give-and-take, humor, and bravery may make a child look disruptive, perhaps even being labeled the class clown.

Student behaviors are directly connected to their everyday classroom performance. Different teachers have different opinions about the usefulness or acceptability of certain behaviors. In addition to grades, behavior benchmarks are often used to explain student success or lack of it. Parents read these in elementary level report cards and narrative reports for older students. Here are some examples taken from report cards I have seen. The lack of strength is shown in parentheses. *The italicized text shows an interpretation that may also be true*:

- Grade 2: "Isaiah struggles to share classroom materials." (Not showing generosity) ...*but might be good at keeping track of resources needed for classroom work*

- Grade 4: "Darla is impulsive in social settings." (Not showing self-regulation) ...*but might be excited or a bit anxious about social interactions*

- Grade 6: "Jordan doodles during class." (Not showing focus) ...*but might be using this strategy to support attentive listening or visualizing*

- Grade 8: "Harley repeats similar patterns in writing." (Not showing creativity) ...*but might be refining skills that can be applied to writing in other areas*

- Grade 10: "Uma gives up easily when problem solving." (Not showing perseverance) ...*but might be managing frustration tolerance well by taking breaks*

Especially if your child is struggling, framing your child's problems as the lack of strengths can sound critical and feel personal at any age. This can give school outsized power in children's lives, casting shadows on strengths they could tap for success. It can be helpful to look for what may also be true, particularly if it shows the behavior as evidence of a possible strength.

The Strength of Knowing Yourself

In the context of school, it may appear that some students lack useful strengths. Teachers sometimes put the spotlight on what is missing, which can become a painful burden for children. Parents can lighten this weight by helping their children see strengths across contexts and beyond academic performance. This is a more holistic view and shows children what is also true and valuable about them.

My daughter's middle school teacher did not value selective attention and self-determination as strengths, and she incorrectly believed that only full attention with focus on activities she controlled would lead to success in her class. But I could see that success was happening for my daughter. It was even evident in grades the teacher herself awarded.

In high school my daughter had a teacher with different strengths. He placed great emphasis on homework and preparation rather than on full classroom attention. He believed that only by producing detailed notes would students be able to pass the AP exam for the subject he was teaching. He took that particular responsibility very seriously.

Despite earning 100% on every weekly practice test and passing the actual AP exam with a high score, my daughter earned zeros for missing homework. She had not completed any of the notes he required. None. The cost of this was quite steep at a time when grades really mattered to her GPA. The teacher, who valued fairness and obedience, was unmoved by her argument that she understood the topics well and had demonstrated mastery in all of the course's assessments. Her grade? D+.

Was my daughter irresponsible or smart? It did not matter. That grade was her consequence for violating the rules and being unwilling to prepare as required of all students in the class. From the teacher's point of view, it was all about fairness to others. But my daughter felt strongly that she did not need to do what he required in order to be successful with AP assessments. To her, the penalty seemed inappropriate and unnecessarily harsh. She stood her ground, showing the strength of standing up for her own beliefs.

How would you have felt about your child not following the rules concerning homework? Proud...or perhaps mortified? Would you have:

- Seen strength of character or only embarrassing and oppositional behavior?

- Intervened by pulling an all-nighter, madly taking notes alongside your child?

- Appealed to the teacher to make an exception?

Listen to your background noise. Your answers will depend on whether you believe that the strength of fairness means all students should have to do exactly the same kinds of work as their peers. Instead, you may believe that it is appropriate for teachers to choose different approaches with different students. The answers to these questions are not always clear-cut. The irony of standards and equality is that they can sometimes limit equity. This means that some students will not get what they need, at least not when they are in school.

Understanding their own learning processes can help students develop their strengths. Sometimes they may have to pay for strengths that they are not willing to sacrifice using, especially when they have a longer-term perspective and a powerful "No!" voice inside. Their strengths may cause trouble, at least in the short term, like that faced by Nikhil (Chapter 7) and my daughter. As you observe them navigating out of difficulties, you discover new perspectives on their strengths. A technique presented in Chapter 11 can help you gain perspective by picturing impacts in the immediate, intermediate, and distant future.

Trouble in the short term does not always mean trouble in the long term. My daughter became a National Merit Commended Scholar, scored one question away from perfect on the SAT Critical Reading, and graduated from high school with both music and theatre awards as well as academic scholarships. She had taken mostly honors and AP courses and still had an impressive GPA despite that one grade. She attended a large private research university, double majored in Film and History, and minored in English Literature. All those AP credits she had earned made it possible for her to complete her bachelor's degree in three years. This gave her an extra year to be a paid intern, to travel extensively, to work internationally, and to test-drive the world of work before picking a career and attending graduate school.

Magnify Strengths at Home

During adolescence, a time when social comparison is very intense, some students feel that they are responsible for and limited by the expectations of teachers. Other students push back and reject what seem to be unreasonable rules. There is a tendency for schools to teach students to value extrinsic control, that pleasing others is the goal. This tendency can actually discourage student engagement by limiting the types of strengths that children consciously use and value at school. It can send the message that being smart is something you are or are not, as judged by others. A more constructive view is that being smart involves a personal collection of strengths that students can develop, refine, and enjoy for themselves.

Your child needs to be aware of their own strengths and choose to use them in ways that work for them in different contexts. Here are actions you can take to spot and build strengths at home, along with example statements you might make:

1. Help your child see their strengths by offering prompt, positive, and incremental feedback.
   Try: "I love the way you _____. (persevered, asked good questions, looked up words you did not

know, created different approaches, were brave, asked for help, told the truth...)"

2. Help your child reflect on the way their strengths work for them, discussing both what worked and what might need adjustment.
   Try: "_____ looks like it went well. What is good about _____? How could you do this another time? What would/can you adjust?"

3. Discuss together barriers that can be tweaked by using strengths.
   Try: "Do you have everything you need to get started? If _____ happens, then you can use _____ strategy or tools."

4. Help your child understand the ways that their strengths show up outside of school.
   Try: "I see your _____ (perseverance, consideration for others, bravery, honesty...) on the sports field."

CONCLUSION

Children succeed at school when they develop character strengths alongside academic skills. Strengths can show up as resourcefulness, managing behavior, and effective learn-to-learn processes. Alert parents can notice the strengths that belong to their children whether or not those strengths are appreciated at school. Some strengths need to be dialed up or down to match the needs of particular contexts. Building a language to talk about strengths and then using that language to help a child see their own strengths in action can help them direct their own future decisions and behaviors.

INKLING 10

I Learn to Appreciate My Strengths

Like most young people, I desired recognition for the ways I used my strengths. I also wanted even more opportunities to grow and use them meaningfully in my work. This turned out to be very challenging in some school contexts, especially in my student teaching, as described in Inkling 5. There, the strengths below were viewed as challenges to the status quo rather than gifts to be developed.

- Creativity = Approaching problems with originality. "What has not been tried yet?"

- Improvising = Flexibly adjusting during the process. "Try this piece."

- Independence = Doing things without supervision. "I'll do it myself."

- Innovation = Creating tools for doing things in new ways. "How might this work?"

- Flexibility = Not needing to do things the same way each time. "Ok, let's try it."

- Helping = Compassion and empathy. "I am with you."

At the boarding school where I learned to teach students with dyslexia, these strengths were incredibly valuable. This work opened my eyes to see that my strengths were valuable for successfully educating children with learning disabilities.

Whatever they may have lacked, my students learned to be inspired by their own potential rather than embarrassed by their bewildering failures. With the right strategic and, yes, artistic teaching approaches, these children were successful. *Creativity. Improvising. Independence. Innovation. Flexibility. Helping.* I was beginning to see how the strengths that showed up on my career assessment were assets.

My future story was not something that I strove toward with single-minded focus. Instead, it revealed itself in small chapters and seemingly random scenes while I lived and worked on it in the present. Many of these meaningful moments were unexpected. Some were undesired at the time they happened. Only in reflection was I able to see that my life's work and my purpose resulted from many meaningful occurrences that were writing my future story for me as I lived it.

With perspective I can tell you exactly how my strengths drove me and sometimes repelled me at work. I can show how I used them in every job I have had since I first began working at age twelve. But in early adulthood while I was still building my identity, I had not connected them to my future story.

When I was about to graduate from college, my career counselor told me I should be an artist. I took a very narrow view of what "artist" meant because I thought I knew all about an artist's job. I did not believe that I had the necessary skills or strengths. It turned out that I did.

CHAPTER 11

Help Students Find Allies and Make Decisions

As your child grows up, they need to become independent. That means making important decisions for themselves and finding other allies besides parents. This chapter helps you support their independence. You can help them spot true friends and mentors. It also describes an important perspective-taking skill that you can help your student learn so they can put crucial decisions in a broader perspective. Allies and the ability to make crucial decisions provide stability in the transition to college and the world of work.

It's OK to Need Help

We all need allies, whether they break spells of learning struggle, deliver superpowers of unconditional love, or create opportunities for a different destiny. Finding allies is not the result of magic. It's more like recognizing that a happy circumstance has delivered somebody especially useful and even wonderful to you or your child.

Fortunately, you and your child have likely acquired some allies along the way who have steered you through stormy weather, shared skill magic with you, and helped both of you to rewrite your difficult life scenes for happier endings. Who would you go to in a crisis? Chapter 5 explored the allies you gathered for yourself. This chapter is about helping your child recognize their own allies. It's no longer all up to you, but you still have a role to play.

The Mentor Ally

A mentor is an ally who has been there, done that. They are seasoned and wise, not just in the ways of work but in the ways of life. What makes this person an ally, though, is not just their ability to connect an older adolescent to opportunities that potentially pave the way to a future profession. A mentor can also connect a young person's possibilities to their bigger life purpose. Often a mentor provides their own hard-won practical knowledge to help a young person try on the world of work. To a parent, this work may look like a fun distraction or even procrastination. To a young person, the mentor provides affirmation of their abilities without the *Why don't you just* questions that even patient parents hear in their background noise, whether they say them out loud or not.

When many parents have run out of rational explanations to convince their older adolescent that a part-time job or an internship would be a great thing to have on a resume, the mentor may have seemingly magical power to convey the same message. To the adolescent, it may sound very different.

The mentor is a helpful expert who is not particularly worried about how the young person will arrive in the future. Ideally, a mentor will have significant industry experience or skills in an area where a young person has an interest or a special skill. Even more than other types of allies, it is critical that the mentor have no conflicts of interest.

Boundaries and Integrity: What a Mentor is Not

Having a mentor can crystalize the imagination of a young adult who struggles to bridge the usefulness of school subjects with a future in which they could feel valuable and happy in the world of work. The young person enters into the mentor arrangement out of their own free will. Sometimes this happens very slowly and grows out of a previous relationship as the child develops an interest in the mentor's field or skills. Very importantly, while parents may have a perfect person in mind to mentor their child, a mentor is never an agent of parents or an organization. A mentor is not in conflict with parents, nor do they occupy the parent ally role described in Chapter 5.

The mentor has clear boundaries. They receive no direct financial or social benefits from mentoring. Such benefits would cloud the guidance of a mentor and compromise their value. Being a mentor means both caring about the young person and having no preconceived idea of how a young person's future might turn out. A mentor is in no hurry to make that future happen for the young person. They also have no attachment to the end result, whether the young person is successful in their pursuits or chooses an unrelated path.

Becoming a Mentor: Walter and Cal's Story

Walter made a living by repairing appliances in his garage. Vacuum cleaners of any make were his specialty, but Walter patiently tinkered with anything he thought he could get to work better. In his neighborhood, he was called the "bike whisperer." No one remembered when the first child stopped by to have a seat raised or brakes tightened, but everyone knew Walter would be in his garage on Sunday afternoon with door up, available to make adjustments. Walter's garage was also a safe place to take apart and reassemble life.

Cal was a regular. His first real bike had been adjusted and repaired so many times that it had become a project, not just a type of transportation. The garage was a respite from Cal's school troubles which often seemed exceedingly hard to repair. Whereas Cal could spend hours getting the spokes perfectly balanced, the brake cables smoothly lubricated, and the gears on his bike realigned, it was too frustrating to fix writing and word problems. Walter saw quite a bit of himself in Cal, the child who was talented with tools and could envision in his mind's eye how to fix and improve nearly anything.

What started as a neighbor relationship became a mentoring one. As Cal grew older and more skilled, he became curious about Walter as a person. "Why, since you are so smart, creative, and good at making things work even better, didn't you go to college? If you could do it over again, what would you have done differently?"

Walter's honest answer was, "I don't know, because that's just me. I make things work." No teacher or parent ally could have done for Cal what Walter did. Cal knew then that he wanted to make things work, too.

As a high school senior, Cal was able to choose half-year elective courses for the first time. He picked one called Hands-on Physics and another called 3-D Design. In these classes he earned his first A grades. The work was project-based and hands-on. Students worked in teams. Cal began to see connections between schoolwork and his future story. He could do what he really cared about, redesigning things so that they would work better than before, as a career.

There were some barriers to achieving this goal. Cal's math record was not robust enough for him to apply to design engineering programs right out of high school. When Cal complained, Walter spoke openly about his own school struggles. Yes, this was something he would have done differently. He'd wished he had gotten more education and been more accepting of help.

Cal took a gap year and worked at a part-time job as a mechanic's assistant. He learned on the job about engines and how parts were machined for them. When the shop owner took Cal to the company that machined their parts, Cal got to see firsthand how parts could be redesigned to work better. He completed the math courses he needed to apply to a college program in design engineering through a local community college. In design engineering school, he discovered that there were other smart, creative people who had also struggled in school. College instructors found Cal very receptive to feedback, willing to spend long hours in the shop, and both polite and personable. These social strengths helped to pave the way to solid recommendations for internships. Cal thanked Walter for years of practice.

How to Spot a True Mentor Ally

Here are some of the qualities that characterize a true mentor:

- They make abstract work become real, especially through hands-on experiences.

- They provide opportunities for an adolescent to try out their interests more deeply, through repeated or playful practice.

- Their mentoring is unpaid and independent of any other adult influence.

- Their own story is not a mirror but a window to be opened at the right time when the young person asks.

- They see and focus on developing the positive attributes and unique skills that the adolescent also likes and values in themselves, especially ones that might be overlooked in an academic environment.

- They help a young person connect the dots from presently enjoyable activities to viable future stories.

Making a Hard Decision: 5-10-50 Thinking

When adolescents have to make a hard decision that may have big impacts on their future stories, I find it helps for them to use what I call *5-10-50 Thinking* to gain perspective. That means getting children to imagine the impacts of a decision at several future times to understand what it will be like to manage through a range of impacts that play out over time.

In Chapter 10, my daughter made the decision to skip what she thought was unnecessary homework. That choice had a huge short-term cost, a D + in the course. Some decisions can thus have devastating near-term outcomes, but in the long term they might not matter in truly important ways. In the grid below my daughter asks herself whether to do her AP homework or not, and extends the impact of the decision over 5-10-50 days, followed by 5-10-50 years, just to be sure.

Table 16: My Daughter Uses 5-10-50 Thinking

Problem: Should I do AP homework?	Imagined Possibilities Over Time
What will happen if I don't do homework (over days)	**5 days:** Nothing. It's not graded till June. (Got 100 on all tests) **10 days:** Nothing. It is not graded until June. (Got 100 on all tests) **50 days:** Maybe a lower grade and a different college choice, but I will have passed the AP exam, still had a strong GPA, and graduated.
What will happen if I don't do homework (over years)	**5 years:** I will have graduated from college a year early and will be traveling the world. **10 years:** I will have a real job, an apartment, and be 27 years old. **50 years:** I will be 67 years old (yikes)
Decision	Don't do homework for this class

The projected times involved in making a hard decision can overlap. This makes choices quite challenging for adolescents, even if they have clear goals.

Here is a 5-10-50 perspective plan for a different problem that doesn't need such a long runway. Alisa is in middle school and doesn't want to play soccer anymore. She is still considering her decision and 5-10-50 thinking helps her see that she is not quite ready to choose:

Table 17: Alisa Uses 5-10-50 Thinking

Problem: Should I quit the team or stay?	Imagined Possibilities Over Time
What will happen if... I quit the team? (over days)	**5 days:** Everyone will gossip about me and say I'm a quitter. I will look like one and be all over social media. **10 days:** I will feel anxious and might have lost some friends. **50 days:** I will be in high school, happier, and have moved on. I will have found a different activity.
Decision	It looks like quitting will be ok over time. Need to be sure I really do not want to play anymore. One more practice and game, then time to decide.

All children need to be able to imagine the impact of a decision at some future period and then work backwards to gain perspective on what it will be like to manage through a range of possible outcomes. This kind of perspective taking can also be used for a very short time frame to slow down and prevent what could otherwise lead to an impulsive decision. Imagine your child having a strategy for that!

Teachers and Parents as Mentoring Allies: Riley's Story

Eleventh-grader Riley sat hunched in the chair facing the head of school's desk. She was still a little intoxicated. Riley's head was swirling. She was about to face a moral dilemma and an adversary with powers far greater than her own. Riley needed an ally.

With great trepidation, heart pounding, Riley made her one phone call to her home, and her father answered. She did not give too many details about how she had happened to be in the head of school's office. Time after time, her father had said if she ever needed him, for any reason, she just needed to call, no questions asked. Riley knew there would be a lot of questions this time, so she told him that she needed a ride.

The head of school, Dr. Z, liked Riley and wanted to help. But this was a major infraction of school rules, and Riley had broken the law. The scene was still unfolding, and the police had been called. Riley's parent was on the way. Dr. Z slowly made small talk about the evening without calling Riley out directly. She asked questions and gave ample wait time. Sometimes drunk students took time to answer.

"Nice to see you, Riley. How was the fall dance tonight? What did you think of the DJ? This one is new to the school. Which of your friends did you get to see? Aren't you the goalkeeper for the soccer team? Great season you've been having. Really impressive."

At first Riley shrugged her answers. She was coherent enough to know that Dr. Z was being oddly nice considering that coming to a school function drunk was not ok.

The ten minutes it took for Riley's father to arrive seemed very long. He was remarkably calm when he entered the office escorted by one of the dance chaperones. Before he took a seat, Riley's father approached the chair where she was sitting and gently kissed the top of her head.

"Hey, Riley," he said with warmth as he moved his chair next to his daughter's chair and waited for Dr. Z to speak. He knew some important things about being a parent ally:

- Broadcast that you are reasonable, open, and that your child has your unconditional love.

- No pre-emptive strikes: Do not defend or deflect your child's behavior.

- Do ask, "Can you say more about that?" a clarifying question that can reveal the other person's position and their openness to continuing dialogue.

Dr. Z saw a very scared *and* very loved young adult before her. She softened her approach somewhat.

"Riley," she opened as she recounted the known facts, "I have been told that you and some friends arrived at school smelling of alcohol. I am going to ask you some questions about when you arrived. Do you think you can answer these questions?"

Riley loosened her teeth from her lower lip and looked at her father. "Yes," she said.

"Riley, who brought you to the dance tonight? Who was with you when you came to school for the dance?"

This, Riley knew, was the moral dilemma: rat out her friends and lose the trust of her peers or refuse to tell and lose the respect of the adults who loved her and wanted to see her successful. In the short term, at least, which is all that most teens can imagine, Riley could see no positive outcomes. Dr. Z was very patient because she knew that Riley was facing the dilemma of adolescence: "Will I align with my peers or with my adult future?"

Riley Uses 5-10-50 Thinking

Riley was not given a plea bargain as she sat in Dr. Z's office. She did not know what would happen to her if she ratted on her friends, though she knew she would be turned overnight from cool to cringey, having committed the ultimate adolescent betrayal. But Dr. Z was in no hurry to extract the answer from Riley, who was very tired and sobering up. Dr. Z. reached behind her and grabbed two bottles of water for her guests and deftly shifted the conversation to the soccer season, what Riley's plans were for the spring team, and if she had her eye on playing in college.

Riley looked at her father and started to cry. Her father returned a searching glance. It was her decision. She knew that she could not lie now, and whatever the consequences were, she could face them.

Table 18: Riley Uses 5-10-50 Thinking

Problem: What will happen if I tell the truth?	Imagining Possibilities Over Time
What will happen if I tell the truth? (over days)	**5 days:** Everyone expelled. Social media train wreck. **10 days:** Different school. Grounded for life. **50 days:** I may have no friends. But they might be expelled. Could I stay?
What will happen if I tell the truth? (over weeks)	**5 weeks:** Friends expelled but maybe I can stay? **10 weeks:** Spring soccer. Will I have defenders? **50 weeks:** Next year: I will apply to colleges. Maybe early decision.
What will happen if "I tell the truth? (over years)	**5 years:** I will have finished college. **10 years:** I will be traveling the world. **50 years:** I can't imagine what I'll be like then.
Decision	I will provide the names of the others involved.

Riley did provide the names of the students who were with her that night. When they were questioned individually, all of them lied. They were expelled. Dr. Z let Riley stay. This reward for her honesty included agreements on Riley's part to cut off contact with the students who had been expelled. She felt it was both a very harsh and a very lucky lesson.

Dr. Z was being a teacher ally. She was designing a learning opportunity and betting on Riley to be mature enough, despite breaking the rules and the law, to make the better decision. Riley quickly used 5-10-50 thinking to decide what to do.

Riley made the high honor roll the next three semesters and graduated with honors and scholarship money. Her college application essay was about moral dilemmas. Dr. Z, a very experienced teacher ally, had engineered a save for this goalkeeper. Riley did get to play soccer in college, where she majored in Business with a concentration in Organizational Behavior.

The Friend Ally

Beyond doing their own laundry, there is a long list of challenges that most new college freshmen have to negotiate as they learn to live relatively independently from their parents. For most students, college will mean enormous amounts of freedom. School will no longer be an all-day event controlled by parents at home and teachers at school. There will be virtually no one else to structure what will feel like endless free time.

When students enter the lab of young adult self-discovery on a college campus, they need to navigate developmental as well as learning challenges while living in a new community.

College freshmen need to be able to engage in what can be a daunting number of tasks.

- Apply academic skills to learn new subjects

- Advocate for themselves effectively

- Use consistent yet adaptable self-regulation practices in an environment with few boundaries or immediate consequences

- Accept the need to self-impose effective structure and routines across health and wellness as well as academic behaviors

- Learn beyond the classroom, both avoiding danger and taking resilience-building risks

- Identify real friends and move on from depleting relationships

Their greatest fear is usually not that they will struggle to manage time and academics, but that they will fail to find their friend group.

Starting Over: Building New Friendships in College

Students have often spent their entire school careers preparing to attend college. Some of the learning, however, will feel like starting over. Even if they have been in varying constellations of friends in high school, once they begin the transition to college, almost everyone on campus will be a stranger.

Students who have met peers at overnight camps may have already had the experience of sharing sleeping and living quarters with someone outside of their family. For others, college will be the first time they'll be sharing a room with a stranger. Armed with an orientation schedule, a meal plan, and opportunities to connect with other incoming freshman, a student's first task will often be to make friends with their roommate.

In an atmosphere of newly limitless possibilities, the dorm room is an important place for creating a friend ally of the stranger sharing their room. To navigate the dorm-room relationship, students need to make decisions for themselves about how to get their needs met. They might call or text you to get answers, but realistically, a parent's most effective help may happen by asking questions. Remind yourself, *Ask, don't tell*. Independently managing the roommate relationship can build self-awareness, boundary setting, and negotiation skills, as well as true friendship.

Roommates need to discover together answers to some of life's biggest questions, such as:

- Can I enter this room at any time, or will it sometimes be off-limits?

- Will I be faced with using earplugs to sleep because my roommate doesn't like to use headphones when they play their guitar?

- Will my underage roommate use illegal drugs or drink alcohol?

- Where will overnight guests sleep? Whose shampoo will they use in the morning? How long can they stay?

- What if my roommate's significant other moves in part way through the semester?

- Who will be responsible for cleaning what, and how often will this happen?

- Will it be ok to borrow and share food and personal belongings?

- How will we compensate or pay when things are lost or broken?

- How will differences be settled? Commit to working it out? Make a contract? Visit residential life staff? Move out?

Friendships Enable Radical Self-Learning

Especially during the first year, when things are new for everyone, college is a powerful time to find friends in the campus community. Real friends are honest, trustworthy, and kind companions. Your child can have spontaneous fun with them, as well as treat them as serious confidants. Real friends will safeguard secrets unless the other is in danger. They can be accountability partners who will push one another toward goals.

Making and keeping friends is complicated. Of all the allies, the friend will probably be the hardest one to develop and maintain. Underneath the specific questions about getting along, bigger questions are being answered, like these:

- What makes me happy?

- Who do I want in my life?

- What are my values? What can't I accept? Where can I bend?

- How might I change? Who am I becoming?

- Who do I want to be? What do I want my life to be like?

Helping Your Child Become Their Own Ally

One of the most important benefits of the gift of self-direction happens once your child is living away from home where they will inevitably face the lure of novel experiences, bolstered by the powerful tug and immediacy of enthusiastic peers. On some occasions, it will be necessary for them to resist exciting opportunities in favor of studying or work responsibilities. Other times, it will be important to accept invitations to try something new. In situations like these, your child can become their own ally.

This is a good time to remember that the risks they take can lead to greater resilience, though you will hope these risks are balanced by judgment and responsibility. It is also a good time to remember to ask non-judgmental questions that let your child know you are interested and there to help, but you also know the decisions are their own to make. It's time to take a backseat and watch where they choose to drive their lives.

CONCLUSION

Raising a child to adulthood means having many opportunities to withhold judgment about their choices. Decisions your child makes without you will also reveal that they are becoming able to establish their own values and goals. You can support them by acknowledging the choices they make, asking questions that are curious rather than judgmental, and remembering that their lives are their own to live rather than an extension of yours. Perhaps you will see yourself among the internalized examples of people they admire and trust.

INKLING 11

My Mentors See and Enhance Strengths

When I was in graduate school, I had two very different instructors. One had innovative and experiential classes but expected turned-in assignments to follow an explicit rubric. Points were awarded for doing exactly what the directions said. The other instructor lectured and facilitated discussion among students who participated and took notes. It was fairly traditional.

The assignments for that second class, however, were much more open-ended and encouraged deep personal exploration of the course materials. The instructor wrote personalized comments and gave extra points for creativity. This instructor was my favorite, and I poured extra effort into every research paper, presentation, and class discussion.

Years later, many of those hands-on experiences from the first instructor have stuck with me. Some of them even shaped my habits of mind and my professional philosophy. What I remember most about graduate school, though, is what it felt like to have that second instructor honor my creative spark. He saw my strength and valued it.

I attended the University of Pennsylvania for graduate school when I was in my forties. I turned down the volume on my own *What if?* background noise as far as possible. With great enthusiasm I became the first learning specialist to earn the Master of Applied Positive Psychology degree. I chose to study with the pioneers of this field to sculpt my view of students' learning and emotional development. I feel very fortunate that exceptional teachers came into my life, especially ones who showed me new ways that my strengths could be channeled into emotionally and practically sound strategies for student success.

Participating in this program gave me all three gifts: new skills, chances to choose items from a whole new world of research to apply in my work, and a self-directed path that gives my life a deep sense of meaning and purpose.

CHAPTER 12

Challenge the Effort Myth

Instead of believing the effort myth, you can choose to believe that your child would try differently if they knew how. That opens the door to using your parent strengths to give the three gifts of motivation that together support your adult child's future as they use their strengths with resilience and growing independence in an uncertain world.

Learning is For a Lifetime

Each learner, at any age, can take actions that work to uncover even more of their potential. Your child has a unique collection of strengths. Developing them can take your child far beyond better grades and academic performance. Your adolescent needs to feel they have at least some choices, that work is about more than just grades or money, and that the stakes are not so high that fear of being judged by people they want to please looms just beyond every attempt.

Beyond the content of school classrooms and curriculum, the world is becoming more complex. Pivot. Shift. Leverage.

Your child will need to develop personalized and agile approaches for lifetime learning and success that will extend far beyond their college years. Although school ends for most people in early adulthood, learning is never completed.

What is your child's future story? It is positively unknowable, and that is exciting. If your child lives for 85 years, fully 80% of their life will be spent outside of formal schooling. As people continue to live longer, knowing how to learn becomes even more essential.

Who is There to Help?

Struggling learners may feel without allies at school, at home, or in the community to help them make sense of learning. Students may internalize their feelings, becoming anxious, depressed, or both. They may also externalize their feelings by acting out, tuning out, or dropping out. They may self-medicate or give up the struggle altogether.

It is understandable that you may want to believe that more effort is the answer. It would be so easy if things could just turn around.

Finding the right professionals, the ones who can address your child's real challenges, is important. You want teachers, coaches, and clinicians who are skilled at identifying your child's strengths and turning them into strategies that meet their needs. When this happens, learning becomes exciting and engaging, rather than full of disappointment, frustration, and suffering.

Keep Giving the Benefit of the Doubt

A student can never forget that their teachers and parents are evaluating them on their school performance. Some children, especially ones with learning, attention, or executive function challenges, may need to ask numerous questions to get to the end of multistep assignments. They may need checklists to follow. Some children just need an answer quickly before they forget why they asked the question in the first place.

Students need praise for what they have done right as well as some help getting back on track when they get lost. What they do not need is to be shamed in the form of reminders that they have not measured up to everybody else and that they should be able to figure it out themselves. If that had worked, even on some level, they would not have reached out.

Heroes of Your Own Story

You and your child can be the heroes of your own stories. As in any myth, the hero faces challenges and conflict. In your hero story, you can raise a resilient, motivated, and independent young adult, sometimes overcoming great odds to do so every day. In their stories, children gain the competence, choice, and self-direction for lifelong learning, powerful relationships, self-awareness, and the motivation to shape their own careers. Together you can successfully face unavoidable stormy weather with superpowers of love, patience, creativity, sacrifice, and flexibility.

What kind of person do you hope your child will be five or ten years from now? Together you can imagine their future story and see them fast-forwarded beyond the present. You and your children do not need to have *the* future story. Remember that you can embrace a forecast that is sometimes unclear without being baffled by your own background noise. Writing a future story involves trying things out, perhaps abandoning some things and modifying others, and later joining pieces that seemed unconnected earlier on.

Wherever you are in your parenting journey, today you can make a difference. It is never too late and it is never too early to get started. I hope this book has helped you see your child's struggles differently, and that you will use core parenting skills for approaching them with more coach-like curiosity. Appreciate that what looks like lack of effort on the part of your child may actually be their best attempt for now. Remember, too, that now is momentary in the *5-10-50 Thinking* of life.

The tools in this book can guide you to help support your child. They are ones to revisit over and over. Your everyday small steps, along with your child's risks and reattempts at learning, build their foundation for growing in abilities, confidence, and self-direction. May they become resilient, motivated, and independent lifelong learners!

Acknowledgments

Writing a book takes the vision, hard work, talents, and dedication of many people besides the author.

I'd like to thank my intrepid editor, Kathryn Britton, for her practical and creative insights, as well as for her uncommon generosity, exceptional wisdom and kindness. Without her this book might never have been completed.

I'm also grateful to Theano Coaching Writers' Workshop and to my colleagues and friends there. They encouraged my outpouring of words and shared my vision for them to become a book. To Senia, Leora and Brian, my early readers, to Kim, who understands all of it, and to Jessica who knew how to jump right in, I thank you.

To my Mastermind colleagues Bailey and AJ, I thank you for your continuing friendship, wisdom, and encouragement beyond our first meetings. Thank you, Lisa for warmly holding the space, and Danny for seeing with the brightness of beginner's eyes. To Lara, Darlene, Beth, Syd, Cecilie, and Ben, I'm grateful for your listening as well as your wealth of ideas.

Thanks go especially to Diana Needham, Business Book Shepherd extraordinaire, whose intricate knowledge of book building, marketing, and positioning turned a manuscript into what you are holding. With the collaborative support of Carla Green, Clarity Designworks' interior book designer and magician, my imagined book became real.

To my Beta readers, Tyra, Karen, Susan, Julia, and Aren, your honest input helped turn a powerful set of connected stories into an even better book.

I'm especially grateful to Meg and Iain, who read and re-read their own stories with new eyes; to Liza whose keen design sense girded early versions of the content; and to Dan who surprised me by not only cooking but also cleaning up.

For my lifelong friend Kerry, I send you buckets of gratitude for every bit of truth and encouragement, and for making and sharing space within and without, in every kind of weather.

Thanks to Pam for including me in your family's celebrations despite COVID, and for flowers, which make everything better.

To Willis and Paul, thanks for listening to and inspiring this neighbor with your authenticity and hands-on help.

Marci: Can you believe it? I'm so glad that I finally took your advice to "Write that down!" I cannot even imagine this book happening without you.

Thank you in a bucketload goes to Sulynn, Nick, Sandy, Kevin, Marie, Marcia, Viriam, Pam, Jenny, and Ruth-Anne for your positive energy, enthusiasm, good humor, encouragement, and loving kindness, always.

To Ty, Henry, and Gloria, your warmth, fuzziness and unconditional love are my dependable happiness and gratitude boosters.

Special thanks to Martin E.P. Seligman and the founders of the field of Positive Psychology. Some of the many researchers and clinicians whom I've had the pleasure to meet or study with, and who continue to inspire my work in the field include: Jer Clifton, Edward Deci, Ed Diener, Angela Duckworth, Jane Dutton, Carol Dweck, Robert Emmons, Jane Gillham, Adam Grant, Jonathan Haidt, Edward Hallowell, Scott Barry Kaufman, Christopher Peterson, Tayyab Rashid, Timothy Pychyl, John Ratey, Karen Reivich, Richard Ryan, Lea Waters, and Amy Wrzesniewski.

All of my clients are special to me in some way, and every one of them has shaped my perspectives about learning and life. I am honored to be included in the lives of Ari, Beth, Cindy, Dave, David, Edlyn, Mary, Maria and Vajra. Your love and admiration are the daily inspiration for why I do this work. Especially to my clients of any age who are still on their own path to self-discovery, remember: *It is not how hard you try that leads to success; it's **how** you try hard that matters most.*

Books Authored or Co-authored by Sherri Fisher

*Unleash Your Epic Self: The Guide to Crushing it
at School, Work and Life*

Positive Edge Journal
Character Strengths Matter: How to Live a Full Life
(Shannon Polly and Kathryn Britton: Eds.)

Resilience: How to Navigate Life's Curves
(Senia Maymin and Kathryn Britton: Eds.)

Gratitude: How to Appreciate Life's Gifts
(Kathryn Britton and Senia Maymin: Eds.)

*SMART Strengths: Building Character, Resilience
and Relationships in Youth*

About the Author

 Sherri Fisher has dedicated decades to challenging the Effort Myth, both in schools and private practice. She believes that no one should have to suffer to be able to learn. Parents who work with Sherri in their youth return with their own children. Her client relationships don't just span grades; they span generations.

As a learning specialist and executive coach for students and their parents, Sherri has pioneered research-based tools that build skilled resilience, motivation, and self-direction. As a schools consultant she has guided educators and administrators to nurture the flexibility, strengths, and relationships that help improve academic and life outcomes.

Sherri is the Director of Learn & Flourish, an education coaching and consulting firm with clients on five continents. She earned her Master's degree in Applied Positive Psychology from the University of Pennsylvania where she studied with the founders of the field. Sherri lives in New England where she raised her children, her gardens, and her big pack of friendly dogs.

Give the Three Gifts of Motivation

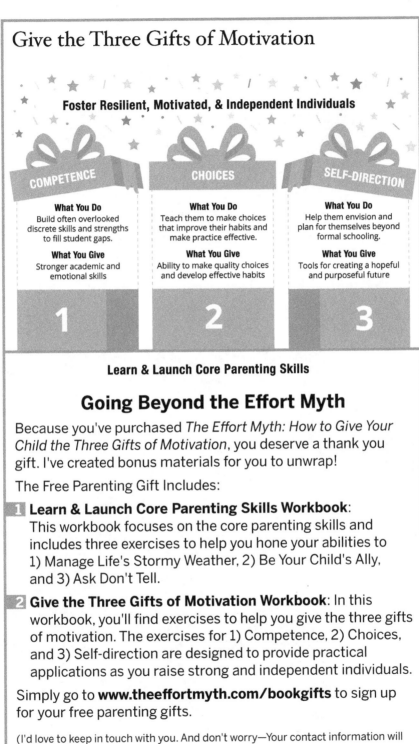

Foster Resilient, Motivated, & Independent Individuals

COMPETENCE

What You Do
Build often overlooked discrete skills and strengths to fill student gaps.

What You Give
Stronger academic and emotional skills

1

CHOICES

What You Do
Teach them to make choices that improve their habits and make practice effective.

What You Give
Ability to make quality choices and develop effective habits

2

SELF-DIRECTION

What You Do
Help them envision and plan for themselves beyond formal schooling.

What You Give
Tools for creating a hopeful and purposeful future

3

Learn & Launch Core Parenting Skills

Going Beyond the Effort Myth

Because you've purchased *The Effort Myth: How to Give Your Child the Three Gifts of Motivation*, you deserve a thank you gift. I've created bonus materials for you to unwrap!

The Free Parenting Gift Includes:

1 Learn & Launch Core Parenting Skills Workbook: This workbook focuses on the core parenting skills and includes three exercises to help you hone your abilities to 1) Manage Life's Stormy Weather, 2) Be Your Child's Ally, and 3) Ask Don't Tell.

2 Give the Three Gifts of Motivation Workbook: In this workbook, you'll find exercises to help you give the three gifts of motivation. The exercises for 1) Competence, 2) Choices, and 3) Self-direction are designed to provide practical applications as you raise strong and independent individuals.

Simply go to **www.theeffortmyth.com/bookgifts** to sign up for your free parenting gifts.

(I'd love to keep in touch with you. And don't worry—Your contact information will never be sold or shared with anyone, and you can unsubscribe at any time.)

CPSIA information can be obtained
at www.ICGtesting.com
Printed in the USA
LVHW081916260122
709251LV00015B/436

9 781732 136816